RESOURCE BOOKS FOR TEACHERS

series editor

ALAN MALEY

D0470574

VERY YOUNG LEARNERS

Vanessa Reilly & Sheila M.Ward

OXFORD
UNIVERSITY PRESS

80354

Oxford University Press
Great Clarendon Street, Oxford OX2 6DP

Oxford New York
Athens Auckland Bangkok Bogota Buenos Aires
Calcutta Cape Town Chennai Dar es Salaam
Delhi Florence Hong Kong Istanbul Karachi
Kuala Lumpur Madrid Melbourne Mexico City
Mumbai Nairobi Paris Sao Paulo Singapore
Taipei Tokyo Toronto Warsaw

and associated companies in
Berlin   Ibadan

Oxford and *Oxford English*
are trade marks of Oxford University Press

ISBN 0 19 437209 X

© Oxford University Press

First published 1997
Third impression 1999

Typeset by Wyvern 21 Ltd, Bristol

Printed in Hong Kong

Acknowledgements

The authors wish to thank the following people for their help and support:

The team from Oxford University Press, who guided us through the publishing process and made many useful suggestions.

Ruby Frost, who contributed ideas.

The CELTE Department at Warwick University.

Vanessa would like to thank Rafa, her family, and friends for their patience and encouragement.

Four anonymous readers who made invaluable comments on the draft manuscript.

The publishers and authors would like to thank the following for their kind permission to reproduce extracts from works published by them.

Stainer and Bell Ltd. for 'Tall shops' © Stainer & Bell Ltd., London, England.

Juliet Moxley for salt dough recipe from *'She' 150 Things to Make and Do with Your Children*

Marie Robinson for 'Pull, pull, pull the cracker – Bang'

Contents

The authors and series editor   1

Foreword   2

Introduction   3

How to use this book   10

Activity	Age	Time (minutes)	Aims	
1 The creative classroom				13
Syllabus and lesson planning				13
Organization of the classroom				15
Classroom language				16
Activity types				17
1.1 Using a story-book	All	Variable	Listening, speaking, vocabulary; stories	21
1.2 Using a video	All	Variable	Listening, speaking, vocabulary, following a story	22
1.3 The princess in the castle	All	10–15	Fairy-tale vocabulary, imagination, drama, co-operation	27
The classroom and what it contains				28
1.4 House register	All	15 + 20	Names, colours, *Where's …*, co-ordination, co-operation	34
1.5 Class monster	All	15–20 +5–10	Vocabulary, drawing	36
1.6 Class mural	All	30	Names, pencil control	37
2 Basic language activities				39
Lively activities				39
2.1 Roll the ball	All	5	Questions, motor skills, co-ordination	39
2.2 Pass the ball	All	5–10	*My name's …*, etc., co-ordination	40
2.3 Go and find a …	All	5–10	Instructions, vocabulary	41

Activity		Age	Time (minutes)	Aims	
2.4	Fetching	All	5–10	Instructions, vocabulary	41
2.5	Pointing	All	5–10	Instructions, vocabulary	42
2.6	Drawing on the board	4, 5, 6	5–10	Parts of the body	42
2.7	Simon says	All	5	Parts of the body, listening	43
Calming activities					43
2.8	Classifying	5, 6	10–15 + 5–10 + 5–10	Instructions, vocabulary, cognitive development	44
2.9	Recognition	4, 5, 6	5–10	Instructions, vocabulary	45
2.10	Find the odd one out	4, 5, 6	5–10	Instructions, vocabulary, cognitive development	47
2.11	Spot the difference	4, 5, 6	5–10	Instructions, vocabulary, cognitive development	48

3	**All about me**				49
Songs and rhymes					49
3.1	What's your name?	All	10–15	Names, confidence	49
3.2	Where are you?	All	10 +	*Where is …?*	51
3.3	Birthday cake and song	All	10 +	Numbers, ages	52
3.4	You've got me	All	5–10	Parts of the body	54
3.5	If you're happy and you know it	All	5–10	Feelings	55
3.6	My favourite toys	All	15	Toys, *I love …*	58
3.7	I am a robot man	All	10	*I can*, action verbs	60
3.8	Five currant buns	All	5–10	Numbers, food, likes/dislikes	61
3.9	The wheels on the bus	All	5–10	Families, transport	63
3.10	Here we go looby loo	All	10–15	Parts of the body	64
3.11	I've got a lot of pets	All	10–15	*I've got, I like …*	66
3.12	Body rhymes	All	5	Parts of the body	68
3.13	Jelly on a plate	All	10–15	Food, likes/dislikes, stress	69
3.14	Pat-a-cake, pat-a-cake	All	5–10	Pronunciation, stress	70
3.15	I like toys	All	10–15	Toys, stress, likes/dislikes	71
Games					72
3.16	Step forward	5, 6	5–10	*Have got*, families, listening	72

Activity		Age	Time (minutes)	Aims	
3.17	Change places	5, 6	1–15	Listening, colours, likes, etc.	73
3.18	Robot game	All	10	Listening, actions	73
3.19	The gingerbread man game	5, 6	15–20	Numbers, parts of the body	74
Stories					75
3.20	The gingerbread man	5, 6	15	Action verbs, listening	75
3.21	Spot's birthday: the book	All	10–15	Listening, animals, *Where is …?*	77
3.22	Spot's birthday: the video	All	10	Animals, *Where is …?*, observation	79
Art and craft activities					80
3.23	Faces—an information gap activity	4, 5, 6	10–15	Parts of the face, listening, giving instructions	80
3.24	Pizza faces	4, 5, 6	20	Food, parts of the face, listening	81
3.25	My family	All	15	Families, drawing	82
3.26	Make a bus	4, 5, 6	15–20	Families, transport, co-ordination	82
3.27	Make a robot	All	20–30	Parts of the body, co-ordination, creativity	83
3.28	Cook a gingerbread man	All	20–30	Parts of the body, manual dexterity	84
3.29	Gingerbread man puppet	4, 5, 6	10–15	Instructions, action verbs	86

4 Number, colour, and shape

					87
Songs and rhymes					87
4.1	Ten green bottles	All	10	Numbers	87
4.2	One, two, three, four, five	All	5	Numbers	89
4.3	Ten little teddy bears	All	5–10	Numbers	90
4.4	One little bird	All	5–10	Numbers, instructions	92
4.5	Red and yellow, pink and green	All	10	Colours	94
4.6	Colours for you	All	10	Colours, weather	95
Games					96
4.7	Please, Mr Crocodile	All	5–10	Colours, asking permission	96
4.8	Gone fishing	All	5–10	*I've got …*	97
4.9	The shape bag	4, 5, 6	10–15	Shapes, colours	98

Activity		Age	Time (minutes)	Aims	
4.10	What's the time, Mr Wolf?	4, 5, 6	10	Numbers, telling the time	99
Story					100
4.11	Red hen and brown fox	All	10–15	Listening, *going to*, *will/won't*	100
Art and craft activities					102
4.12	Teddy bear face prints	All	10–15	Instructions, co-ordination	102
4.13	My favourite colour	All	15–20	Colours, instructions	103
4.14	Pockets	4, 5, 6	15	Colours, instructions	104
4.15	Colour mixing: magic glasses	5, 6	10–15	Secondary colours	105
4.16	Plasticine shapes	All	10	Shapes, instructions, manual dexterity	106

Activity		Age	Time (minutes)	Aims	
5	**The world around us**				108
Songs and rhymes					108
5.1	In and out the shops and houses	All	10–15	Town vocabulary, action verbs, greetings	108
5.2	Beep beep beep	All	10	Colours, road safety, pretend play	110
5.3	Sirens	All	10	Emergency services	112
5.4	It's raining, it's pouring	All	5–10	Weather	113
5.5	Animals	All	10–15	Animals, adjectives, *it likes*, action verbs	114
5.6	Tall shops	All	5	Town vocabulary	116
5.7	Incy wincy spider	All	5	Weather, *up*, *down*	117
5.8	The weather	All	5	Weather	118
5.9	Miss Polly had a dolly	All	5–10	*Doctor*, *sick*, *pill*, talking about illness	119
5.10	Ladybird, ladybird	All	5	Wildlife	121
Games					122
5.11	Going to the doctor's	All	15	Illness, role-play	122
5.12	Traffic lights	All	10–15	Colours, instructions	123
5.13	Sirens game	All	10–15	Emergency services, listening, pretend play	124
5.14	Weather game	All	10–15	Weather, clothes, instructions	125
5.15	Animal movements	All	10–15	Animals, action verbs, listening	126

Activity	Age	Time (minutes)	Aims	
Story				127
5.16 The hare and the tortoise	All	10–15	Animals, comparatives, listening	127
Art and craft activities				129
5.17 Weather mobile	4, 5, 6	20	Weather, instructions, manual dexterity	129
5.18 Raindrop people	All	10	Instructions, colouring	130
5.19 Spiders	5, 6	10–15	Instructions, manual dexterity	131
5.20 A ladybird	4, 5, 6	10–15	Instructions, co-ordination	132

6	**Festivals**				133
Christmas					133
6.1	Twinkle twinkle little star	All	10	Traditional song	134
6.2	O Christmas tree	All	10	Christmas and weather vocabulary	135
6.3	I'm a fairy doll	All	15	Toys	136
6.4	Here is the tree	All	10	*Tree*, *green*, *box*	137
6.5	Pull the cracker	All	10	Rhythm	138
6.6	Guess the present	All	15	*What is it?*, shapes, colours	139
6.7	Make a Christmas tree	All	20	Colours, co-ordination	139
6.8	Christmas star	4, 5, 6	20	*Star*, instructions, co-ordination	140
6.9	Nativity play	All	Several lessons	Drama, confidence	141
6.10	Crackers	4, 5, 6	20	Instructions, co-ordination	143
Carnival					144
6.11	Carnival song	All	10	*Mask*, *costume*, etc., *going to*	145
6.12	Pirate hat	All	15–20	Instructions, co-ordination	147
Easter					149
6.13	Hot cross buns	All	5	Instructions, food, singing	149
6.14	Story: Why do rabbits have long ears?	All	15–20	Listening, animals, *I'm a …, you're a …*	151
6.15	Animal masks	4, 5, 6	15–20	Animals, colours, co-ordination	152

Activity	Age	Time (minutes)	Aims	
6.16 Can you find the eggs?	All	5–10	*Where is/are ...,* prepositions, observation, colouring	153
6.17 Egg and spoon race	4, 5, 6	15	Action verbs, co-ordination, team game	154
6.18 Egg painting	All	15	Colours, instructions, co-ordination	155
Photocopiable worksheets				156
Flashcards				177
Further reading				187
Index of topics and language points				194

The authors and series editor

Vanessa Reilly is a teacher at London Centre, Seville, Spain. She is also a freelance teacher trainer who gives sessions for the Centro de Profesores in Seville, and other in-service training including language improvement sessions for English teachers. She has taught many levels and age groups. She has an M.A. in Teaching English to Young Learners (with distinction) from the University of Warwick (U.K.). She is currently writing a primary course book for OUP.

Sheila Margaret Ward has taught in various countries and has worked with students of all ages from very young learners to adults. She is at present a teacher with the British Council in Lisbon, Portugal. She is the author of *Dippitydoo* (Longman), a book of songs and activities for children, and she composed the songs for *Pyramid 3* (Escolar Editora).

Alan Maley worked for The British Council from 1962 to 1988, serving as English Language Officer in Yugoslavia, Ghana, Italy, France, and China, and as Regional Representative in South India (Madras). From 1988 to 1993 he was Director-General of the Bell Educational Trust, Cambridge. From 1993 to 1998 he was Senior Fellow in the Department of English Language and Literature of the National University of Singapore. He is currently a freelance consultant and Director of the graduate English programme at Assumption University, Bangkok. Among his publications are *Literature*, in this series, *Beyond Words*, *Sounds Interesting*, *Sounds Intriguing*, *Words*, *Variations on a Theme*, and *Drama Techniques in Language Learning* (all with Alan Duff), *The Mind's Eye* (with Françoise Grellet and Alan Duff), *Learning to Listen* and *Poem into Poem* (with Sandra Moulding), and *Short and Sweet*. He is also Series Editor for the Oxford Supplementary Skills series.

Foreword

The publication of this book reflects the growing demand for English teaching to pre-school age children worldwide. Although research findings on the optimal age for foreign language learning remain inconclusive, this does not deter parents around the world, who not only perceive English to be the language of opportunity for their offspring, but who also wish them to have access to it at an ever younger age.

This demand has given rise to a mushroom growth in private lessons for very young learners in many countries, in addition to public nursery school or kindergarten education. As demand increases, a major problem arises in the supply of adequately trained and appropriately experienced teachers. Often teachers with primary school training but with little English are enlisted. In other cases, teachers with ELT qualifications but no experience of teaching this age group may be used.

Clearly there is a crying need for the 'professionalization' of this new field of language teaching. Very young learners, who will usually be pre-literate, and who inhabit a world quite different from that of their elders, require special handling. The emphasis will more often be on guiding the children's overall development than on the specifics of the language, which may be no more than an incidental bonus. The authors of this book have drawn on their long and extensive experience to offer a framework of support for teachers entering this exciting new field, as well as additional material for those who are already in it. The book will be an invaluable complement to the already published *Young Learners* in the same series.

Alan Maley

Introduction

This book aims to provide activities for children which have a language bias and which are based on sound pre-school practice and educational theory.

Who is this book for?

Very young learners

In this book 'very young learners' refers to children who have not yet started compulsory schooling and have not yet started to read. This varies according to the country and can mean children up to the age of seven, so we have taken three to six years as a realistic average. What counts more than chronological age is the developmental age. This will vary according to the individual and the help and encouragement he or she has already received, either at home or in the nursery.

The children may be attending state or private nursery schools or kindergartens, and the school may teach English as a foreign language or may be an English-medium school where English is taught as a second language. Alternatively, the children may be attending private English classes outside school. The classes may be very large or very small.

The children may have had some exposure to English, or may be absolute beginners. Children learning English as a second language (ESL) may be in classes with native speakers. At the age we are dealing with, this should not be too much of a problem as native speakers are not yet proficient in their own language and still have a lot to learn.

There may be some disparity with regard to basic skills such as drawing and cutting and this needs to be borne in mind constantly.

Their teachers

There is a growing trend in many countries for children to start their language learning at a much younger age. This means that many teachers who trained to teach adults and teenagers are finding themselves with classes of very young learners. At the same time many primary and pre-school teachers whose first language is not English are being asked to teach English too.

In addition to these teachers, who have to adjust their teaching methodology, there are teachers who are in the process of being trained to teach a foreign language to early learners.

This book provides advice and ideas for all these groups of teachers.

Smoothing the way

Whether the children are new to school or simply new to the English class, there are various ways in which you can help them to adapt. It would be ideal if you could visit them in their own homes before the term starts, but this is often not practicable. Alternatively, you can invite the children, with their parents or guardians, to a little pre-term party so that they can get to know their teacher and class-mates in a less formal setting. If the parents or guardians speak English, they can stimulate the child's curiosity by using it at home. You can also invite parents or guardians to attend lessons and even help.

Use of the mother tongue

It is obvious that if the children come from a variety of linguistic backgrounds or if you do not speak their language, you will have to use English as the medium of communication. In other cases, the school or education authority may insist that you do not use the mother tongue in the language class. However, many teachers are not told specifically whether they should use the mother tongue or to what extent, and consequently they are uncertain what to do for the best.

Although the ultimate objective is to use only the target language in the classroom, we feel that there is some justification for using the mother tongue, especially in the early stages. The reasons are as follows:

Security

For anyone of whatever age, learning a new language is a traumatic experience. Some language learners, like some swimmers, can be thrown in at the deep end and survive. For others the experience is so nerve-racking that they form a block. Small children, who have spent their time among loved and trusted people, need some time to adjust to the school environment. If the strangeness of a new school and unknown faces is compounded by having someone jabbering at them in a foreign language, the experience must be terrifying. For this reason it can be helpful to put them at ease by speaking to them in their own language and gradually weaning them on to using more and more English in class.

Need for communication

Children are desperate to impart information, some of which may be totally inconsequential to adult listeners but which is of great importance to them. Communication is a vital part of the learning process but if we tell the children they can only speak in English (which of course they cannot do) it is as good as telling them to be quiet. This would be a great shame in terms of the teacher–pupil relationship. Furthermore, you can use some of the things they tell you as a springboard into vocabulary or other language work, and to help you relate activities to their interests. What a child says can also give useful feedback about how the child feels at school or even at home.

Giving instructions

We may want to organize a game or explain how to make something. We often spend a long time trying to get the message across in English (and probably failing) when a couple of words in the mother tongue would make everything clear. At this stage you can give the instructions first in English and then in the mother tongue. Later on, when the children are familiar with the procedure and English phrases, you only need to use English.

Avoiding the mother tongue

Gesture

Gesture is an important tool, particularly with very young learners, who still rely on body language and facial expression to communicate. You can accompany instructions, stories, songs, and rhymes by actions, pictures, and mime to show the meaning. Some cultures have a wide variety of gestures which they use when speaking, which you can exploit if you are familiar with them.

Using English words that are similar to the mother tongue

Where possible, it may be useful to use English words that are similar in the child's own language. For example, if you teach children who speak a Romance language you may say 'Very good' followed by 'Excellent'.

However, by doing this we may be encouraging children to choose the easy option rather than helping them to use an expression which would be more natural for a native speaker. There is also the danger that they will assume that every English word which is similar to one in their own language has the same meaning, as they are unaware of 'false friends'. Never the less, we feel that the advantages in terms of getting instant understanding and instilling confidence in the children outweigh the disadvantages.

Using international English

Nowadays many English words have been absorbed into other languages, for example, *taxi, hamburger, T-shirt, jeans, cinema*. By using some of these words we can make the learning of a new language easier.

English hats

In order to signal to the children when they must use English, you could put on a special hat, which could be any type of hat, cap, beret, or even a paper one, but should always be the same one. You tell the children that this is your 'English Hat' and that when you are wearing it you cannot speak or understand anything but English. You could extend this by getting the children to make their own English Hats out of newspaper (see 6.12, 'How to make a pirate hat'). When they are wearing their English Hats they can only speak English to you and their class-mates.

Dolls and puppets which 'only understand English' are another effective way of encouraging children to speak in English, and can help to reduce inhibitions. On the other hand, some children have no inhibitions and always want to show off what they can do.

Some teachers find that speaking English encourages the children to speak more English. However, if English is not your native language you may not be very confident about using it in class. There is some guidance on classroom English on page 17 in Chapter 1, and in the activities classroom language is given in *italic* print.

Learner characteristics

Individual attention

It is very important that small children get the teacher's individual attention as much as possible. Some will demand it by clambering on to your knee or holding your hand, but others need it just as much.

A good opportunity to give them individual attention is when they are drawing or colouring. At this point you can go round talking about what they are doing and maybe eliciting some vocabulary. It is often at this point that children will say if anything is worrying them.

Attention span

For the teacher used to an older age-group it can be quite disconcerting when a three-year-old wanders off in the middle of a song or story to play with a toy. It does not mean they are not following what is going on; it is probably because some other child had the toy before and they see this as their only opportunity to get hold of it. We must not take it as a personal rejection. It is very difficult to hold the attention of a whole group of small children and the best way to do it is to ring the changes every five to ten minutes—unless you see that they are all really absorbed in what they are doing, in which case you can let it go on a bit longer.

It is a good idea to make a note of the things they really enjoy and which you know will get the attention of the whole group. This age-group love what is familiar and may seem indifferent to something new. By this we do not mean that you should never try anything new. On the contrary, what is new in one lesson has become familiar by the second lesson. Do not be put off when children do not readily accept an activity the first time; it is worth persisting with something you feel they will eventually like.

The 'silent period'

It is important for the language teacher to remember that young children may spend a long time absorbing language before they actually produce anything. It is not a good idea to try to force them to speak in the target language as this can create a lot of emotional stress. Even if small children are not actually saying anything, they will still be taking it in. Some children say nothing at all in class but go home and tell their parents what they have learnt. By doing repetitive songs, rhymes, games, and plenty of choral work, children will be able to produce language without the stress of having to speak individually.

Pre-school teaching

There are certain advantages in teaching the pre-school age group. One of the main bonuses for the teacher is that there are usually no strict syllabuses to follow, no tests, and no performance objectives to be met. Anything the children learn is a gain and this absence from pressure means that the classes can be an enjoyable experience for both teacher and pupils. Things do not need to be rushed and if the children enjoy a particular activity, it can be repeated over and over again.

Another advantage is that children of this age are less inhibited. They are not afraid to be imaginative and they are not yet bound by the constraints that demand that adults be logical. As they are so young, they are not carrying any negative attitudes left over from previous school experiences. They are curious about everything, keen to learn, and very receptive.

There are, of course, some difficulties to be faced when teaching very young children. They can be selfish and uncooperative. If they want something, they will push another child over to get it and show little concern for the other child's feelings. Some of them will use temper tantrums to try and get their own way, and may scream or bite. Some may need help with going to the toilet and there could be occasional accidents with incontinence.

If a child seems withdrawn, bad-tempered, or upset, talk to the parents (or to the class teacher if this is not possible). Very young children can be strongly affected by events at home such as a new baby or moving house.

Needless to say, an enormous amount of patience is needed and some days you might get the feeling you have hardly taught them anything because it has taken so long to organize them. However, if you have been using English, they will have been learning even if you have not done a single thing on your lesson plan.

Child development and language teaching

During the pre-school years children develop better eye–hand co-ordination, their pictures become more recognizable and detailed, and they learn to do simple craft activities which involve cutting, sticking, and folding. They learn to do simple jigsaw puzzles and activities which involve recognizing similarities and differences. They learn how to sort, classify, and match things, and recognize the 'odd one out'. They are starting to learn to count and to have a concept of quality, position, size, and amount.

They are able to follow a story, predict what might come next, and ask questions about it. They can use their imagination to invent their own stories. This is the stage at which children often have an imaginary friend, and they sometimes find it hard to separate fantasy and reality. They enjoy looking at books with pictures and will often pretend they are reading the text, even when they cannot decipher the individual words. This stage often gives way naturally to real reading if children have enough contact with books and a person willing to read the stories again and again.

Children of this age are still rather self-centred and may often want to play alone and may not want to co-operate with the group. This will gradually disappear with gentle encouragement and as the desire to socialize becomes stronger. At this age children can begin to take part in organized games, although they may not be very good losers.

The role of the teacher during these pre-school years is to help the child develop in all these areas and to prepare the ground for the more formal kind of teaching that will come in primary school. Much of the learning will take place through play. It is widely recognized nowadays that play is an important part of the learning process. Childish games of 'let's pretend' help children to rehearse for the real world and give them an opportunity to try out situations in order to learn to cope with them. Other games help to develop conceptual awareness, physical co-ordination, creativity, and social skills.

The implications of all this for the language teacher are that the main emphasis should be on the type of activities which children normally do at pre-school, adapted to language learning. Activities most suited to very young learners are those which involve songs, chants, rhymes, stories, total physical response (see below), tasks that involve drawing, colouring, cutting and sticking, games, puzzles, dressing up, acting, and 'let's pretend'.

Total physical response

Pre-school children learn through direct experience via the five senses, and do not yet understand abstract concepts. For this reason language teachers find it very useful to use what is known as 'Total Physical Response' (TPR). This means getting the children to actually do or mime what we are talking about. If a teacher says: 'Alexander, open the door, please' and Alexander opens the door, that is an example of total physical response.

The younger the children are, the more important TPR is. You can use it in many ways: for example, by getting the children to follow instructions in a game or craft activity, in miming a song, rhyme, or action, or in acting out a role-play.

How to use this book

How the book is organized

The book is divided into six chapters: 'The creative classroom', 'Basic language activities', 'All about me', 'Number, colour, and shape', 'The world around us', 'Festivals'. The topic areas and activities have been chosen on the basis of children's development from the familiar (self, home, school) to the outside world, and reflect what teachers would normally be covering in a pre-school class.

The book does not provide a complete course in English for very young children, but seeks to provide ideas and guidelines which you can use to develop your own syllabus and lessons (see Chapter 1, pages 13–15). You can adapt them to suit your children's age, development, culture, etc. For example, you could use the same ideas with a different song, game, or festival. The Variations provide some ideas for this.

Small children are very egocentric, so we have placed most emphasis on 'All about me' (Chapter 3), which deals with the identification and description of self, and likes and dislikes. Chapter 2, 'Basic language activities' and Chapter 4, 'Number, colour, and shape' are concerned with developing children's conceptual awareness, their eye–hand co-ordination, and their motor skills. Chapter 5, 'The world around us', extends the children's horizons and includes such topics as the town, traffic, the doctor, the emergency services, animals, and the weather. Chapter 6, 'Festivals', includes Christmas, Carnival, and Easter as examples of festivals that are fun for small children. You can of course add or substitute other festivals as many of the activities are suitable for other occasions.

Each chapter is divided into the following areas: 'Songs and rhymes', 'Games', 'Stories', and 'Craft activities'. There are cross-references between activities on the same topic and ideas for links and follow-ups.

The Further Reading section at the end of the book gives examples of useful books and stories, games, videos, etc. which are educational and enjoyable. We have given addresses you can order them from if they are not available in your country or region.

How each activity is organized

Age

The activities are suitable for ages 3, 4, 5, 6, or All. The suggestions are only approximate—you know your children best and you must choose what is suitable for them. There could be a wide gap between different children of the same age—for example, some three-year-olds have better motor control than some six-year-olds in certain activities.

We have not given any indications about language level as learning with this age-group should be holistic rather than segmented. Language use should arise naturally from the activities, and language development needs to be integrated with physical and social development. The kind of language a pre-school teacher can use is limited anyway because children of this age do not speak their native language perfectly yet, and still have a limited conceptual awareness. Ideas of too abstract a nature should be avoided and activities should centre around the child's experience of life. Children with varying levels of English should be able to participate in the same activities without any serious problems.

Time

We have suggested how long the activities might take, but it can vary a lot. It will depend on the size of the class, the age of the children, the stage of development of individual children, how much experience the children have had of a particular type of activity, and how many times you wish to repeat certain items (such as songs).

Very young children have a limited attention span and it is important to change activities before they get bored. If necessary you can finish an activity or come back to a song or story in another lesson. This will also provide useful revision.

Aims

The aims of each activity are divided into 'Language' or 'Other'. The linguistic aims tell us what language that particular activity practises, and the 'Other' aims refer to children's physical, cognitive, or social development. Of course you can alter the activity, the aims, and the language to suit your children and what you wish to teach.

Description

The description explains what happens during the activity and provides a quick and easy reference.

Materials

This section lists the things that are needed in order to be able to do the activity. Where no materials are needed this heading is absent.

Preparation

This tells you what you need to do prior to the lesson.

In class

The stages of the lesson are numbered in order to provide a clear sequence to follow.

Follow-up

This gives you some suggestions for activities which could follow on naturally from that lesson. There are also cross-references to other activities in the book.

Variations

Ideas to show you how you can adapt some activities to practise different topics or language, or to suit another group of children.

Comments

This part contains clarifications, comments, or advice on specific points about the activities or the children.

1 The creative classroom

Syllabus and lesson planning

Designing a syllabus

A syllabus for pre-school children will be quite different from one for older learners.

First of all, most children of this age cannot yet read and write, or make the kind of abstract deductions that even a child of seven can make. The children will still be gaining basic skills such as holding a crayon or pencil, colouring in, relating the real thing to a pictorial representation of it, being able to recognize shapes, sorting and classifying, recognizing similarities and differences, using scissors, glue, and other implements. Any syllabus will have to take all these things into consideration.

Whereas older children could be expected to follow a clear structural progression and to acquire some basic grammar rules, small children will learn better by mimicking and using language in context. It is quite normal for native-speaker children to say things like 'I did went' at the age of four or five, and so in the early stages it is better not to worry too much about grammatical correctness but to get the children to enjoy using the language. This is best achieved by topic-led work.

In many countries there is no prescriptive syllabus for pre-school teaching. This has the advantage of giving teachers the freedom to design the syllabus around the children's own needs and interests, but the disadvantage is that teachers have no guidelines as to what they should teach and how they should set about it. We hope that the teaching suggestions contained in this book will help you work out and implement your own syllabus.

How you plan your syllabus and your lessons will depend on your teaching situation, but as far as possible it would be a good idea to link what you are teaching to what the children are learning in their pre-school classes in their own language. If you are their teacher all the time this will be easier, but if not, you may need to liaise with their other teachers and their parents/guardians. It is important to show the children that English is a means of communication and that it can be a vehicle through which they learn other things.

Although this book is divided into topic areas in the order that we consider most relevant to small children, it does not constitute a syllabus and you will need to decide the order in which you wish to present language. A typical order might be:

1 Identification—name (verb—*am, is, are*)
2 Numbers, age (verb—*am, is, are*)
3 Parts of the body (verb—*I've got …*)
4 Colours, Description (verbs—*am, is are, I've got …*)
5 Family (verb—*I've got …*)

This is only a suggestion as there are no hard and fast rules about creating a syllabus. You may find it useful to find out what the latest craze is (dinosaurs, *Batman*, etc.) before planning your course.

With this age-group exposure to a wide range of language through stories, songs, videos, etc. is very important, and we should try to build up a vast passive knowledge (in the same way as children learning their first language). It is vital to remember that the children are very young and that we are aiming to make their first exposure to English an enjoyable one. They have many years of learning ahead of them and they will have enough hurdles to jump later on. If their first experience of English (or any other language) is pleasurable, they will have a positive attitude towards it for the rest of their lives.

If your pupils have had no contact with English before, it is important to start off with simple, basic language and to recycle it in as many ways as possible.

Lesson planning

How much can small children reasonably be expected to learn in one lesson? Although children might seem to have no trouble understanding and using the language being presented, this does not mean that they have learnt it, and only repeated exposure and recycling over many lessons will ensure that they are able to use the language independently. Fortunately, young children like what is familiar and want the same story, song, etc. again and again.

Your lesson planning will depend on your children and how long you see them for. If your lessons are more than fifteen minutes in length, you need to keep the children's interest by changing activities every five or ten minutes. This is why it is important to have a wide variety of activities.

Some children work more quickly than others, so it is useful to have some toys, games, or jigsaws for them to play with, or pictures to colour in, while the other children are finishing.

With small children it can help to have an established routine. It gives them a sense of security and they know what to expect. You can have signals which indicate a change of activity. For example, a whistle might indicate an active game, a piece of calm or classical music the prelude to a story, a clap the introduction to a rhyme or chant. It does not really matter what your signals are but once they become an established routine, it will be easier to organize the children.

A possible lesson plan might be as follows:

1 A familiar song
2 New language
3 Craft activity connected with the new language
4 A song, rhyme, or chant connected with the new language
5 A familiar active game or activities with Total Physical Response
6 A familiar story

You need to have a balance of lively and calming activities (see Chapter 2, 'Basic language activities').

Organization of the classroom

If your teaching situation allows for some flexibility, it is best to have a space in the classroom where physical activities such as dancing and active games can take place. When telling stories, taking the register, etc., if possible seat the children on a carpet in semicircles facing the teacher as this makes communication easier. If your desks are fixed to the floor, perhaps you could use the area between the teacher's desk and the pupils' desks.

It is important to have a place where the children's work can be displayed. If the classroom is used for other subjects perhaps there could be an 'English corner'.

Class management

Children of this age are not used to pair or group work and the activities will generally be whole-class, choral-type work led by the teacher or done on an individual basis. However, it is important that children of this age learn to co-operate. Games, role-play, and joint efforts (see 1.4, 'House register') all contribute to this end.

It is not easy to organize small children into a homogeneous group. In many pre-school classes a large amount of time is spent on free or semi-directed play with just some of the time spent on whole-group activities such as story-telling or singing. There are often helpers to organize the rest of the children while the teacher deals with individuals or small groups.

However, in the majority of schools the situation is very different. Classes are large and teachers often receive no assistance at all. English teachers may see the children for one or more periods a week varying in length between 15 minutes to an hour or more. This means that different strategies will need to be employed according to the situation. Most teaching will tend to be teacher-centred and opportunities for free play will be minimal due to the classroom set-up and the need to expose the children to the target language as soon as possible.

Although some of the work will involve whole-class activities such as choral work, question and answer, chanting and singing, in other activities, such as crafts, the children will be working individually. If there is a mix of ages or abilities it may be necessary to divide the class into smaller groups according to their developmental age and deal with them separately so that while one group is colouring and cutting, for example, another group is listening to a story or doing some specific language practice. This sounds difficult to organize, but it is preferable to forcing some children to do things they are not ready for or boring those who are ready to go on to something more challenging.

If possible, you can use the corners of the classroom as special areas: one corner could have some toys, one could have some games, another could have some picture-books and old magazines and catalogues. If some children have finished their work quickly they could go to one of the corners and play for a few minutes.

When most of the children have finished an activity, they can be involved in something else such as a story or a song while the others have time to complete their work.

Sometimes children just do not want to join in. When this happens, it is better not to make an issue of it. They may be hungry, tired, or anxious about some aspect of the activity. Usually when they see that the others are having a good time, they will want to join in.

If possible, enlist the help of parents who might be willing to participate and help children with going to the toilet as well as setting up craft activities etc. Some might even welcome the chance to learn English!

If you feel that a particular activity is not going well, do not be afraid to change tack and do something you know the children love. You can always come back to the original activity on another day when the children are more receptive.

There will inevitably be a fair amount of noise, especially when the children get excited during an active game. If possible, play some of the games in the school playground or field.

Classroom language

Children can pick up a lot of language through the normal day-to-day routine of what we do in class. Greetings, instructions, etc. should all be carried out in English. From the beginning you can respond in English even if the children use their first language, but gradually encourage them to use English themselves. Non-native teachers of English often ask what expressions they should use. This is very difficult to say as native speakers vary a lot in what they use, but a few of the most common are given below:

Instructions (teacher)

- *Look at me/Listen to me/Could you come here please?*
- *Put your (coat) on/take your (coat) off.*
- *Don't do that/Stop (pushing, picking your nose, etc.)*
- *Quiet, please/Pay attention, please.*
- *Please get into line.*
- *Make a circle/hold hands/drop hands.*
- *Put your hand up.*
- *This is how you (colour, fold, cut, stick, tear) it.*
- *Go and find/fetch me a …*
- *Give me your papers.*

Praising

It is important to praise small children's efforts. Here are some useful phrases:

- *Well done!*
- *Very good.*
- *That's a nice picture.*

Requests (pupils)

- *Can I have a …?*
- *Can I go to the toilet?*
- *Can I borrow a … ?*
- *Can I clean the board/give out the papers/collect the papers?*

Clarification (pupils)

- *What's [hermano] in English?*
- *I don't understand.*

For more examples of classroom language see the books *Use of English in the Classroom* by Sagrario Salaberri or *A Handbook of Classroom English* by Glyn Hughes (see Further Reading, page 187).

Activity types

Story-telling and drama

When we are teaching pre-literate children, we need to revert to time-honoured story-telling skills and use visual aids, dramatic tone of voice, mimicry, gesture, and mime to bring the story alive. You do not have to be good at acting to keep a group of children enthralled. Even though modern children are brought up on a diet of television, they still enjoy the human contact of a real live person telling them a story.

When telling a story, it is important to create a close and intimate atmosphere. The children can sit in semicircles on a carpet or cushions round your chair. This should ensure that your face, hands, and visual aids are visible to all the children.

It is better to tell a story than to read it from a book, in order to create better interaction with the children and to have eye contact with them. You can write down a few cues and these, together with any pictures and drawings, should help you remember the story. Later on, when you want to encourage children to start reading books, it will be a good idea to read some of the stories from books, showing the children the pictures in order to stimulate interest in the books themselves.

From the beginning encourage the children to join in with the story where there is repetition. By the second or third telling you can start leaving bits out or altering the story, which will have the double value of checking on listening comprehension and encouraging the children to speak.

There are many children's stories available, both traditional and modern, and you will probably choose your favourites. It might be better to start off with traditional stories from the children's own cultural background as they may already be familiar to the children and this will aid comprehension. If English books are not available, you can use a book written in the children's own language for the pictures and tell the story yourself. There is a danger of over-simplifying the language when telling a story, but story-books written for native speakers are fine with this age-group and it is essential to expose them to fluent and natural English.

Stories are usually about (imaginary) things which happened in the past, and the stories in this book include past tense forms. Obviously we are not suggesting that you should teach the children how to form tenses such as the simple past or past continuous, but in the context of a story they will hear them and understand them naturally, which is a good preparation for active use when the children are older.

A dramatic way to present a story is by using an overhead projector and creating a shadow-play. The darkened room, the focused light, and the movement of the figures create an atmosphere which has long been appreciated in the theatre tradition. Older children can prepare the cut-outs which are to be used. Alternatively, you can create a shadow-play theatre by hanging up a sheet to act as a screen and shining a strong light behind it.

The children themselves will want to tell stories, often about the drawings they are doing or what has happened to them. You can encourage this by asking questions. Later on, when they are beginning to read and write, they can write and illustrate their 'news'.

At this age children spend a lot of time in a fantasy world, sometimes conversing and playing games with an imaginary friend, sometimes 'being' a cowboy, robot, dinosaur, nurse, superman, etc. The older the child, the more elaborate the creation will generally be. While children of three or four may just play at being a character for a short while, children of six or seven construct an elaborate plot to their game.

This creativity can be harnessed in the classroom by encouraging the children to re-enact stories you have told them. This works particularly well with some of the old favourites such as 'Little Red Riding Hood', 'The gingerbread man', 'The three billy-goats', etc. The children quickly pick up the repeated dialogues and can use them appropriately in their dramatizations. (See 'Pretend play', page 26.)

Some teachers like to tell stories using a felt board and figures cut out of felt, which is a useful way of illustrating the meaning. Nowadays, velcro is a useful material and figures with velcro backing can be stuck to a fuzzy board. If these are unavailable, figures can be stuck on to a whiteboard with sticky tape, Blu-tack, or plasticine. Alternatively, you can use magnets to stick up pictures on some of the modern whiteboards.

With all of these methods the children can help to prepare the characters and to move the figures when you tell the story.

For more ideas and tips, see *Storytelling with Children* by Andrew Wright in this series, which also contains helpful guide-lines for simple board drawings.

Using story-books and videos

Very young children cannot yet read, but it is a good idea to interest them in books so that they want to learn. As well as telling stories from memory, read them stories from picture books. Choose a book which is short and has large, clear pictures. Make sure all the children can see the book and pause to show them the pictures as you are reading.

In Further Reading (page 187) we suggest some books which are suitable for very young children. Some books, for example *Where's Spot?* by Eric Hill and *The Very Hungry Caterpillar* by Eric Carle, are available in many languages and in bilingual versions. If you can't find books in English, use books in the children's language and paraphrase them in English. You can still show the pictures and the children won't know the difference!

Many children's stories are available in both book and video form (and some now on CD-ROM). Some children will be familiar with story characters from TV but not with the books they originally came from. You can use both versions to help the children to understand the story, and to stimulate interest in books and reading. The different media help children to use different strategies for understanding the language.

Videos are an excellent resource and have the advantage of combining stories with animation. They give a lot of language input and it does not even matter if they have subtitles in the pupil's language as very young children cannot read yet.

There is a danger that the children will want to watch passively and although that might be justified when they are very tired, you can do predicting and pre-watching activities with them. For example, before watching a *Postman Pat* episode you can ask them if he has a cat or a dog and what colour it is. You can pre-teach some words so that the children will recognize them in the video.

After viewing, you can ask the children to re-enact a video story, or to draw a picture about it, which can lead to more language practice.

It is not advisable to use long videos or cartoons which simply consist of the characters trying to hurt each other. The best ones are the short episodes produced for children's television. Characters such as Postman Pat, Fireman Sam, Brum, Spot, The Mr Men, and Rupert Bear are very popular with children and have good underlying educational principles. There are some specially-produced videos for teaching English such as *Wizadora*, the *Longman Fairy Stories*, and *Muzzy in Gondoland*, which are also very useful for teaching this age-group.

Here are some guidelines for choosing a video to use in the English class with very young children:

- It should be short (5–10 minutes)
- It must have a good storyline
- It must be suitable for the age-group
- The language should be easy to understand by watching the actions
- Think about what activities you could do to help the children understand it, for example acting it out.

Some children's videos are available in many countries and languages. Some do not have a soundtrack, but are still useful for teaching English. You can talk about what happens and get the children to predict what happens next. But don't forget to let the children enjoy the video story as well as using it to practise their English!

Below are some examples of how to use books and videos in class. You do not have to follow all these steps and they can be divided over several lessons. Children of this age love hearing the same story over and over again.

1.1 Using a story-book

AGE	**All**
TIME	**Variable**
AIMS	**Language:** listening, speaking, vocabulary **Other:** introduction to books, learning to follow a story
DESCRIPTION	The children listen to a story then dramatize it or draw a picture or make a picture book.
MATERIALS	The book.
PREPARATION	Read the book before the lesson and make sure you know it well.

IN CLASS

1 Show the children the pictures in the book and tell them the key words. If the children know the story, let them tell you what they know about it. Give them a chance to speak and then ask questions such as: *How do we say … in English?* Then supply the word.

2 Read the story, pointing to the pictures and dramatizing it as much as possible.

3 Tell the story again, getting the children to act it out while you tell it. Encourage them to use any repeated phrases or easily remembered dialogue.

FOLLOW-UP 1

Get the children to draw scenes from the story. Pin them up on the classroom wall or make a book out of them. (For details on how to make books, see *Creating Stories with Children* by Andrew Wright in this series.)

FOLLOW-UP 2

In another lesson tell the story again. Encourage the children to contribute as much as possible. Pause from time to time to elicit words and ask what happened next.

COMMENTS	See also 3.21, 'Spot's birthday: the book' for an example of how to use a specific book.

1.2   Using a video

AGE	**All**
TIME	**Variable**
AIMS	**Language:** listening, speaking, vocabulary **Other:** following a story
DESCRIPTION	The children watch a story on video and dramatize it or draw a picture.
MATERIALS	A video about 5 minutes long; pictures of some key words in the story.
PREPARATION	Watch the video before the lesson so that you know it well.
IN CLASS	1 Pre-teach some key words from the story. 2 Show the whole video with the sound off. Talk to the children about what happened and elicit some of the key words. If they know the story they may want to comment on it, especially if there are any variations from the version they know. Encourage this kind of participation and introduce some more key words. 3 Tell the children that you are going to show the video again, this time with sound, and that they should listen for some key words. 4 Play the video with the sound on. 5 Ask the children which words they heard.
FOLLOW-UP 1	Get the children to re-enact the story while you tell it. Encourage them to use any bits of dialogue that are easy to remember.
FOLLOW-UP 2	Get the children to draw scenes from the story. Pin them up on the wall or make them into a picture book. Retell the story using the children's pictures.
FOLLOW-UP 3	In another lesson, show the video again. Encourage the children to supply key words. Pause the video at exciting places and ask the children what happens next.
VARIATIONS	There are many ways of exploiting videos to help children learn English. See 3.22, 'Spot's birthday: the video' for another example. Sarah Phillips' book *Young Learners* in this series has a whole chapter on using video (see Further Reading).

Combining a book and a video

Here are a few suggestions as to how a book and a video can complement each other.

- Tell the story using the book first and then back it up by using the video.
- Prepare children for the video by showing the pictures in the book and teaching some key words. Then show the video.
- Show the video. Then tell the story from the book and ask if there are any differences between the book version and the video version. Show the video again and point out the differences.

Songs, chants, rhymes, and music

Songs, chants, and rhymes help children's language development, and also their physical development when used in conjunction with dance and mime.

The language in traditional songs is rich and colourful and extends the children's vocabulary beyond the limited range of their own day-to-day experiences. The use of rhyme encourages children to explore the sounds of words, and the use of imagery enriches their perception of the world and their ability to express what they feel.

Religious practices have long recognized the mystic power of chanting. When words are linked to rhythm and music they seem to have more emotive and personal significance and so are remembered better.

One of the linguistic advantages of songs, chants, and rhymes is that the learners will happily repeat the same structure, even the same words, over and over again without getting bored. Songs, chants, and rhymes are particularly useful in a stress-timed language such as English because the rhythm forces us to put the stress in the right places and to observe the strong and weak forms. At the same time pronunciation is improved as the students are concentrating on sound rather than meaning. Young children are excellent mimics, although you cannot expect perfect pronunciation, especially if they cannot yet pronounce all the sounds of their mother tongue. They are particularly good at copying intonation.

Relatives and friends are always delighted when children can sing or recite in another language and it is useful to have a repertoire ready for end-of-term concerts and other festivities. Teachers often worry about where to find songs, chants, and rhymes, and some suggestions appear under topic areas in this book. However, there is no great secret to turning ordinary language into chants. If you listen to children playing in the yard, it will not be long before you hear something like this: 'Na, na, na, na, na, I'm better than you-ou', chanted in a sing-song voice. An old favourite in the U.K. used to be: 'I'm the king of the castle and you're the dirty rascal.' Children find it quite natural to turn almost anything into a chant. You can fit the words to any topic you are doing. For example:

We're going to the beach (zoo/park/moon, etc.)
We're going to the beach
Hooray, Hooray
We're going to the beach.

You could even encourage the children to make up a little tune to these words if they want to, and to make up new chants of their own.

Another alternative is to take a well-known tune and put your own words to it. Here is an example using the traditional French tune 'Frère Jacques'.

I like chocolate, I like chocolate
How about you? How about you?
Do you like chocolate? Do you like chocolate?
Yes, I do. Yes, I do.

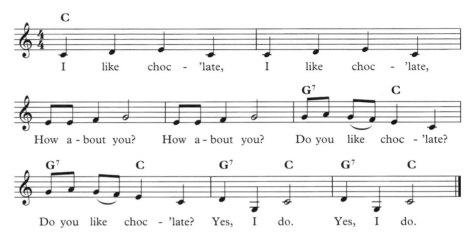

You could invite the children to suggest other goodies for the song, for example, 'I like ice-cream'.

There are several ways in which songs can be taught. You can get the children to recite the words after you and then add the melody later, or you can sing the song and get the children to sing the melody to 'la-la-la'. If the song has a word which is frequently repeated or a sound like 'crash', the children will soon start joining in on those words.

It is better not to try to do too much in one session. The first couple of times, you can play the song and sing it once or twice and encourage the children to join in. There will always be some children who do not sing and it is not advisable to insist on it. If the song is catchy enough and simple enough, they will usually want to sing it.

Most of the songs in this book have actions and you may find that some of the children will start doing the actions before they are ready to sing the song. Some will forget to sing while they are doing the actions and some will find it difficult to co-ordinate both the singing and the actions. The younger they are, the more difficulty they will have. Do not worry if the children do not join in at first as they are listening and doing the actions. They will join in when they feel right.

Most of the traditional songs in this book are available on the *Jingle Bells* and *Super Songs* cassettes published by Oxford University Press, which also contain other songs useful for young children.

Art and craft activities

Art and craft activities are an important part of the pre-school curriculum and need to be a common feature in classes. Children need both free and guided art and craft activities and it is important to provide both.

Craft activities are a very valuable way of giving the children 'comprehensible language input' as they have to listen to instructions in order to complete an activity. Instructions should be given in the target language and supported by a lot of demonstration. It is important not to forget free painting. Children need and enjoy this type of activity. It develops the children's independence and allows them the freedom to choose what they draw. Although there is no specific language being taught, the teacher can go round asking children questions in English about their painting, for example, *Who's this? What is he doing? What colour are you going to paint the ...?*

When doing craft activities it is always a good idea to make things yourself first so that you have an example to show the children. It is also advisable to prepare more materials than you need in case a child makes a mistake and has to start again.

You need enough scissors for each child. At this age they should only be allowed to use the special ones with rounded ends. If the children are very young and not very good with scissors, you can perforate the outline of the picture by going round it with a sewing-machine needle. The machine will take about five copies at a time so it should not be too time-consuming to prepare them. With this method it is easy for the children to break the perforations using their finger-nails. The least messy glue is the sort that comes in sticks, but if glue is not easily available or is too expensive, you can make a paste by boiling up flour and water.

Brushes need to be of medium thickness and paints need to be the sort that wash off easily. Children like felt-tipped pens but they do not have the versatility of paints. They have a short life-span and as children are inclined to press quite hard, they tend to come through the paper. They are also very difficult to get out of clothes. Wax crayons are good for this age group, especially for the smaller ones; however, as children get older and we try to encourage them to be more careful and colour within the lines, crayons become too clumsy. Coloured pencils are better for older children who want to be more accurate. Other materials which are useful are grease-proof paper and carbon paper for tracing, and aluminium foil (see 'Making visuals' on page 31). Old egg boxes, both the plastic and cardboard sort, can be useful, as can old margarine and ice-cream tubs for holding water and other things. You need plenty of paper and cardboard. Old cereal boxes and other packaging can be used for various things. Once your friends and the children's parents discover that you are prepared to recycle these items, you will probably be swamped with materials.

It is very important to display children's work as it gives them a sense of achievement. It is a good idea to neaten the edges of pictures and to mount them in order to make the display look professional. Invite parents to come and view their child's work when they come to pick them up. It is always a good idea to let children take work home after displaying it for a short time, for the benefit of parents who cannot come and see the pictures. It is a nice idea to have an art show for parents and family at the end of term to coincide with school plays or parents' evenings.

Organized games

Games help children to acquire language in the natural way that native speakers do. The language is used as a means to an end rather than an end in itself, and the children are motivated to learn because they are enjoying themselves. Games also teach social skills such as co-operating and obeying rules.

Very young children do not require the sophistication in a game that older children would look for and many simple activities can seem like games to the children and be used over and over again. We have included some appropriate games under the different topic areas, but many simple game-like activities can be used to practise different language items.

It is important to remember a few points when talking about games. Firstly, small children always expect to win and it takes them some time to learn to lose gracefully. For this reason it is better to avoid competitive games with the youngest ones. In an elimination game such as 'Simon Says' you can let them carry on playing once it is clear to them that they did not carry out the instruction. Secondly, children of this age are not well co-ordinated and they find it difficult to throw a ball, to use a skipping-rope, and to catch a ball, so you need to avoid games which require this degree of precision.

If you have a large class of very small children, it might not be wise to do very active and exciting games such as 'What's the Time, Mr Wolf?' as some of them could fall over and get hurt.

Pretend play

It has long been recognized that pretend play is important in a child's development, but recently research has shown that the intervention of an adult in this play can extend the interaction and enrich the language used. It follows that teachers could make use of this natural phenomenon to encourage the use of a second language.

For example, you could tell a fairy-tale story and then encourage children to act out and extend the story and thus develop their fantasy play and vocabulary (see 'Story-telling and drama', page 17).

1.3 The princess in the castle

AGE	**All**
TIME	**10–15 minutes**
AIMS	**Language:** fairy-tale vocabulary **Other:** to develop imagination, drama, co-operative effort
DESCRIPTION	The teacher shows the children how a simple story can develop.
MATERIALS	A mop or brush, some large cardboard boxes.
IN CLASS	1 Use some large cardboard boxes to make a 'castle'. Make a wall with them across one corner of the room. Stand behind them and say: *Help! Help! I'm a princess. I'm a prisoner in this castle.* Then let some of the children pretend to be the princess.

2 Make yourself look fierce and prowl up and down in front of the boxes. Say: *I'm a monster. The princess is my prisoner.* Let some of the children pretend to be the monster. Get behind the wall of boxes again and say: *Help! Help! Who can save me?* Encourage the children to be the princess calling for help.

3 Now the mop can become a horse for the prince. Turn the mop upside down, put your legs astride it, and say: *This is my horse. Her name's (Gina).* Pretend to ride round the room. Let the children take turns at riding round the room and invent their own names for the horse (but don't let them do it for too long). Then put your legs astride the mop and say: *I'm the prince. I'm coming to save you.* Encourage the 'princess' to stand behind you astride the mop and you both gallop across the classroom.

4 Repeat the scene from the beginning and let one of the children be the prince.

COMMENTS	You may find that little girls do not mind being princes, but little boys often do not like taking female parts. If you want to encourage more positive attitudes, you can have the princess rescue the prince next time.

VARIATIONS

You can encourage the children to make up their own variations on the story. Either in the same lesson (if time permits) or in a subsequent lesson, you could ask the children to suggest what other pretend situations you can act out using a horse or a castle. They can then enact the scene. You supply any language needed and help them to extend their ideas if necessary.

The classroom and what it contains

Most pre-primary schools and kindergartens have games and toys, but if you are teaching young children privately or in a school for older children, it may be necessary to improvise. Although children of this age already have a good imagination, it is much more fun to use 'props' such as cups, plates, spoons, knives, and forks for playing at restaurants and a telephone for phone calls. Other useful objects are cars, ships, planes, toy animals, and some dolls.

Building materials

Children of this age enjoy constructing things: houses, towers, etc., and so it can be useful to have building materials for this purpose. Toy building bricks and Lego are popular but old boxes and plastic containers can also be used. You can encourage the children to make things and talk about what they are making. These materials can also be used to help develop concepts of number, size, distance, balance, logical connections, patterns, sequences, categories, and materials, and the language associated with these concepts.

Improvising

A large box from the supermarket with a few extra things we usually throw away can make an excellent pirate ship, ambulance, police motor cycle, truck, puppet theatre, television, or shop counter.

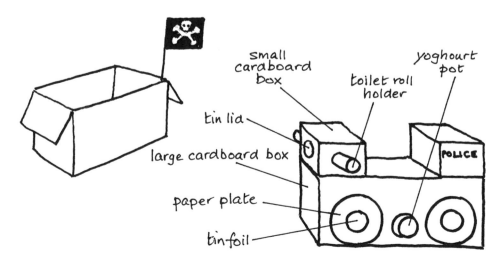

A mop can become a hobby-horse.

Chairs can be arranged as a car or a plane.

Four chairs can be pushed together to make a cage for a zoo.

A rug can be a 'magic carpet', a field, a lake, or a house.

A sheet pinned to a notice-board and weighed down with objects can become a tent. If this is not possible then a sheet draped over the teacher's desk is just as effective.

Materials

It is true that when teaching children we need an endless supply of materials but this need not be expensive. The best thing is to enlist the help of friends, colleagues, the parents of the children, and any local shops that are willing to co-operate. Many printers and paper and cardboard companies have off-cuts—lengths of paper and card which they cannot sell and will give to schools.

Things to ask people to collect

- old Christmas and greeting cards for making collages and decorations
- empty food packets which you can put in a shop
- silver paper (for making robots, spaceships, etc.)
- yoghurt pots to mix paints in, to act as cups in a restaurant, etc.
- old wrapping paper
- old magazines and catalogues
- old newspapers (to cover the floors and desks during messy activities and for papier mâché)
- left-over wallpaper (to draw on, as a base for collage, to cover notice-boards)
- old wrapping paper from presents
- string, wool, thread (hair for puppets)
- bottle tops, lids (to draw round)
- big boxes from shops

Dressing up box

It is very useful to have a dressing up box for role-play, pretend-play, and drama activities. You can collect clothes from family, friends, and parents over a period of time and also make costumes out of crêpe paper.

Making visuals

Many teachers are worried because they cannot draw. When teaching very small children, anything the teacher draws will be better than their efforts and as long as it is recognizable the children will be happy. They are always astonished at what adults can do anyway.

Andrew Wright's *1000+ Pictures for Teachers to Copy* and *The Blackboard Book* by Eleanor Watts give helpful guidance on doing simple board drawings (see Further Reading).

If you feel that you cannot draw even minimally, you can trace pictures from books in the following way:

1 Place a piece of grease-proof paper over the picture you want to copy.
2 Trace the outline of the picture with a hard pencil.
3 Put a sheet of carbon paper on to a sheet of clean paper with the ink side down.
4 Lay your grease-proof paper with the outline on top of the carbon paper.
5 Go over the outline again and the picture will appear on the clean sheet.

If you are tracing from a magazine you can simply put the clean sheet with the carbon paper under the picture and trace round the picture itself with a ball-point pen. If you are lucky enough to have an overhead projector you can simply trace over a picture using a transparency or photocopy on to a transparency. (You will need to be careful with copyright restrictions when copying from publications.)

Creative classrooms

The very young learners' classroom needs to look exciting when the children arrive for the first time. A 'creative classroom' attracts young children who may have reservations about leaving their parents for an alien environment—the classroom. It will impress parents that the children in the school work hard but that the work is designed for their enjoyment too.

The aim of the 'creative classroom' is to use visually stimulating work to arouse the children's curiosity when they arrive. Displays need to be attractive and purposeful and can be used to encourage greater independence (see 1.4, 'House register'). Creating an exciting classroom is not just for the artistic among us; it can be done by anyone, cheaply and in a relatively short time.

For people, stick figures are enough:

You can elaborate by adding clothes:

For animals draw a basic shape and add distinguishing features:

1.4 House register

AGE   All

TIME   **Lesson 1: 15 minutes**
                           Lesson 2: 20 minutes

AIMS   **Language:** names, colours, following instructions, *Where's …?*
                           Other: eye–hand co-ordination, co-operative effort, to encourage independence

DESCRIPTION   The children paint the class register, colour in their names, and learn how to stick their names on and take them off.

MATERIALS   Plain wallpaper or a large roll of paper, paints, trays for the paints (ice-cream tubs, gardening trays, etc.), sponges, velcro with a sticky back or something similar, cardboard, coloured pencils/crayons, old newspapers.

PREPARATION   1 On the paper draw any shape: a school bus, a cottage, a house, a school—depending on what most appeals to your learners (see illustration). It needs to be big enough for the children to stick their names on. Make name-plates for all the children out of cardboard and write their names so that the children can colour them (see illustration). Leave enough space for the children to draw their face next to their name.

2 Before the first lesson lay your picture on some newspapers. Have some paints mixed; only have a little bit of paint on each tray as this way the children will not saturate the sponges.

IN CLASS   **Lesson 1**
1 As soon as the children come in get them sitting round the picture.
2 Teach them the colours you have mixed.
3 Show the children how to colour using sponges. It is best to use sponges as they are quicker than brushes and because there is less pressure to paint inside the lines.
4 The children can now colour the picture using the sponges.
5 Once they have finished put the picture somewhere where it can dry.

Lesson 2

1 Get the children to sit in a circle round you. Hold up one of the name-plates and say, for example, *Where's Ana?* Continue to do this giving out all the name-plates.

2 Tell the children to colour their names with pencils or crayons and to draw their face in the space.

3 Once the children have finished get them to make a semicircle around you and the picture.

4 Show them the velcro and demonstrate how it sticks and unsticks. (Velcro is preferable but if you cannot obtain any, then Blu-tack, plasticine, or something similar can be used. Whatever you use it must be possible to stick it on and take it off on a regular basis.)

5 Cut off a small piece. Ask for one of their name-plates and stick one side of the velcro to it. Then stick the other side to your picture; you could stick it to the 'windows' on the 'bus' or to the 'bricks' on the 'house' (see illustration).

6 Do the same for all the children.

7 Then, with the help of the children, put the picture on the wall.

8 Ask the children to go and stick their name-plates on the picture.

9 In subsequent classes the children register each time they come in by sticking their names on the house. You could keep the name plates in a box on your desk so that the children do not misplace them.

COMMENTS

It is useful to have a register which children can use every lesson to 'check in'. It makes it easier for you to see who is present and the daily ritual of putting up their names will have a double advantage of giving a focus to the beginning of the lesson and familiarizing the children with the written form of their name.

It is probably better to use two lessons to make the register unless you have the children for longer than half an hour.

1.5   Class monster

AGE	**All**
TIME	**15–20 minutes + 5–10 minutes in subsequent lessons**
AIMS	**Language:** to revise vocabulary **Other:** drawing
DESCRIPTION	The children feed the monster with words that are covered in the lesson. The monster only 'digests' those words which have been learnt.
MATERIALS	A monster, pictures to illustrate the vocabulary (at least one per child), card for the children to draw on, Blu-tack.
PREPARATION	Draw a monster with a large mouth and a large stomach. This one is Vanessa's class monster (affectionately dubbed 'Willy' by her pupils).

IN CLASS

Lesson 1

1 At the end of every class (usually the last fifteen minutes) show the children some pictures of the vocabulary covered in class and elicit the English words.

2 Spread the pictures on the floor.

3 Get each child to choose a different picture to draw on a piece of card.

4 The children 'feed' the monster before going home, sticking the cards in her/his mouth.

Lesson 2

5   Remove the cards. Show the children the pictures and try to elicit the words. If they remember a word, the monster digests it and the picture card is attached to her/his stomach. If no one can remember the word the card stays in 'Willy's' mouth.

Lesson 3

6   Go through the same process with the words in 'Willy's' stomach. If the children answer correctly, pin up the 'digested' words around the classroom.

FOLLOW-UP

You can practise classifying words by grouping them on the classroom walls. (See 2.8, 'Classifying'.)

COMMENTS

If you only see the children for a short time each session, then they could feed pictures you have prepared instead of drawing their own.

1.6   Class mural

AGE

All

TIME

30 minutes

AIMS

Language: say their names
Other: to practise pencil control

DESCRIPTION

The children draw their own faces to make a mural.

MATERIALS

Paper, pencils, rubbers, and colours.

PREPARATION

Take a group photograph of the children.

IN CLASS

1   Give each child a worksheet or piece of paper.
2   Ask them to draw their faces in the 'picture frame'. Tell them to draw the faces **big** (emphasizing the size with your hand) as some children draw them the same size as in the photo.
3   Write each child's name on her/his paper unless she/he already knows how to do it. Those who are already starting to read and write may like to copy their own name.
4   Stick the photo you took in the middle of a notice-board.
5   Once the children have finished, ask them to go and find themselves in the photo.
6   Stick their 'portraits' around the photograph and make a pointer with some sewing thread and pins linking their portrait with their photograph (see diagram).

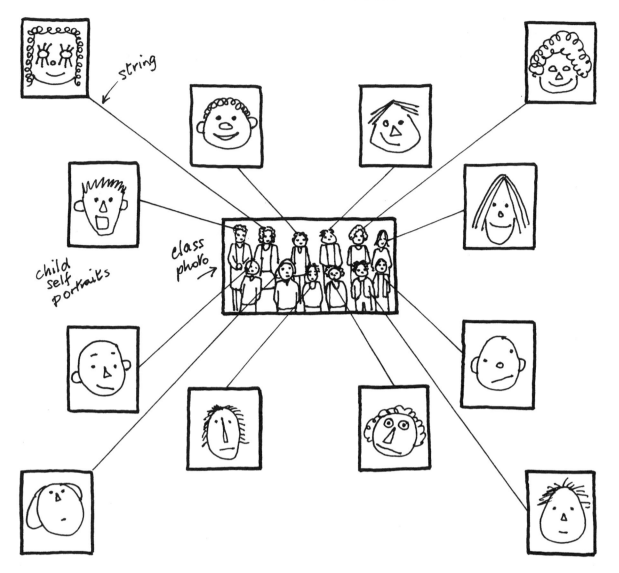

string

child
self
portraits

class
photo

FOLLOW-UP	In subsequent classes you could add to the mural with other information, for example, photos or pictures of their families, their best friend, their likes/dislikes, their favourite food, toys, etc.
VARIATION	As an alternative you could take individual photos as well as the group photo and use those instead of the children's pictures.

2 Basic language activities

There are many activities which seem like games to children but which practise basic language. Most of them can be adapted to fit in with the topics in this book.

We have divided the activities in this chapter into 'lively' and 'calming' activities to help you choose which type you need for a particular stage in the lesson. Little children need to move around a lot and it is unreasonable to expect them to remain glued to their seats for any length of time. Doing a lively activity gives them a chance to move about under the teacher's control and with a specific language aim in view. On the other hand, being able to sit down and concentrate on a task is an important part of their development and necessary for their later studies. Therefore teachers of this age-group need to balance both aspects when planning a lesson.

Lively activities

2.1 Roll the ball

AGE	**All**
TIME	**5 minutes**
AIMS	**Language:** question and answer **Other:** motor skills, eye–hand co-ordination
DESCRIPTION	The children roll the ball to each other, ask and answer questions.
MATERIALS	A small ball (such as a tennis ball).
PREPARATION	Choose which question and answer you want to practise. Spend one or two minutes teaching and practising it.

IN CLASS

1 Get the children to sit down on the floor in a circle.
2 Roll the ball to the first child and ask, *What's your name?* (or whatever question you are practising).
3 Supply the answer (e.g. *Ana*) and then get the child to answer.
4 Indicate that you want the child to roll the ball to another child.
5 Look at the child who has rolled the ball and encourage her/him to say *What's your name?* to the child who received the ball.

6 When the child has asked the question, look at the child who received the ball and repeat the question, encouraging her/him to answer.

7 When the second child has answered, get her/him to roll the ball to a third child, and so on.

COMMENTS

This might seem a bit laborious at the beginning but once the children get the idea they enjoy it very much. If older children are able to throw and catch they might enjoy this instead of rolling the ball.

2.2 Pass the ball

AGE

All

TIME

5–10 minutes

AIMS

Language: whatever language you want to practise. For example, the children could practise saying *My name's …* or *I'm four*, colours, or animals; or you could give an instruction such as *Run round the circle* or *Touch your toes.*

Other: linking music and movement to language

DESCRIPTION

The children pass a ball round while music plays. When it stops, they practise the target language.

MATERIALS

A cassette or record player, some lively music, a small ball.

IN CLASS

1 Get the children to sit on the floor in a circle and give the ball to one of the children.

2 Start the music and tell them to pass the ball from one to the other round the circle.

3 Stop the music suddenly and say *Stop!* Indicate that they must stop passing the ball round.

4 Say to the child holding the ball, *My name's Pedro* (or whatever phrase you want to practise) and indicate that he is to say his name. When he does it correctly, clap your hands and get the others to clap too.

5 Start the music again and get the children to carry on passing the ball round.

6 Stop the music suddenly and get the child who is holding the ball to say *My name's ….*

7 Carry on in this way three or four more times.

COMMENTS

If you have a very large class, only a few children will get a chance to speak but they will all have to rehearse the language mentally in case they get caught with the ball. The excitement of the game will involve them all.

VARIATION	Put pictures of words the children have been learning into a box or bag. They pass this round while the music is playing. When the music stops, they take out a picture and say what it is.

2.3 Go and find a ...

AGE	**All**
TIME	**5–10 minutes**
AIMS	**Language:** to follow instructions, to practise vocabulary, to introduce a useful piece of classroom language
DESCRIPTION	The teacher gives instructions and the children run to the correct picture.
MATERIALS	Pictures of vocabulary items you want to practise.
PREPARATION	Cut out or draw some large pictures of the vocabulary you want to practise. Stick the pictures around the wall before the children come in.
IN CLASS	1 Walk to the first picture and elicit the word or tell the children what it is. Get them to repeat.
	2 Do the same with the other pictures.
	3 Call one child out: *Andreas, come here, please* (beckoning and gesturing). When the child is standing beside you, say and mime, *Go to the bus*. If he does it correctly say, *Well done*. If he is not sure, take his hand and run with him to the bus.
	4 Repeat the procedure with other children.
VARIATION	Older children may like a competitive element. You could call out two children and give them both an instruction, for example: *Andreas, go and find a bus and Mohammed, go and find a plane*. The first one to get there is the winner.

2.4 Fetching

AGE	**All**
TIME	**5–10 minutes**
AIMS	**Language:** to follow instructions, to revise vocabulary
DESCRIPTION	The children listen to instructions and fetch the correct item.
MATERIALS	Some objects or pictures of vocabulary you have already introduced in a previous lesson.

IN CLASS

1 Show the children the objects or pictures and practise the vocabulary.
2 Spread the things and pictures on the floor.
3 Call out one of the children and give the instruction: *Marta, could you fetch me a rabbit, please.* If she has difficulty, go with her to pick up the rabbit and then get her to fetch it for you.
4 Continue in the same way, getting different children to fetch things.

FOLLOW-UP

1 Place the objects or pictures in different places around the room before the children come in.
2 Get the children to go and fetch you things.

2.5 Pointing

AGE

All

TIME

5–10 minutes

AIMS

Language: to follow instructions, to practise vocabulary

DESCRIPTION

The children come out and point to the correct picture.

MATERIALS

Pictures of the vocabulary you want to practise, something to stick them on to the board with.

IN CLASS

1 Show the children the first picture, and teach or revise the word. Then stick the picture low down on the board at child height.
2 Do the same with the other pictures.
3 When all the pictures are on the board call out one of the children and say *Wanda, point to the tree, please.* If the child has difficulty, take her hand and point her finger to the tree.
4 Continue in the same way, calling different children for each picture.

2.6 Drawing on the board

AGE

4, 5, 6

TIME

5–10 minutes

AIMS

Language: to follow instructions, to practise parts of the body

DESCRIPTION

The children draw on the board according to the teacher's instructions.

MATERIALS

Board and chalk or board-pen.

IN CLASS

1 Call out one of the children and tell her/him to draw a head.
2 Call out another child and tell her/him to draw the body and join it to the head.
3 Continue in this way, calling out different children to add the different features until the drawing is complete.

VARIATIONS

This could be done with other vocabulary.

COMMENTS

Children love being allowed to draw on the board using the teacher's chalk or board-pen, and you can turn this to good use in the language class.

2.7 Simon says

AGE

All

TIME

5 minutes

AIMS

Language: listening, following instructions, parts of the body, classroom vocabulary

DESCRIPTION

The children listen and carry out the instructions only when 'Simon' tells them to.

IN CLASS

1 Tell the children that you are going to give them instructions, but they must only obey if you begin by saying 'Simon says'. (You can change this to fit any current popular characters such as 'Robocop says'.)
2 Say the instructions, doing the actions yourself: *Simon says touch your nose. Simon says touch the floor. Simon says stand on one leg.* Then say *Touch your nose* and do not do the action. Normally anyone who does the action without 'Simon says' is out, but with young children it is better not to exclude them from the game. It is enough to look at them, smile, shake your head and say, *I didn't say 'Simon says'.*
3 If you have a child who is very confident and speaks well, you could let her/him give some of the instructions.

VARIATION

See 3.18, 'Robot game', where children obey instructions only when the speaker says 'please'.

Calming activities

These activities encourage the children to work quietly and independently at a task. They help to develop the children's cognitive skills and visual recognition and prepare them for the kind of work they will be expected to do at Primary School.

2.8 Classifying

AGE	**All**
AIMS	**Language:** to follow instructions, to practise vocabulary **Other:** to develop cognitive skills, visual recognition
DESCRIPTION	The children have to recognize which things belong to a particular category.

Lesson 1

TIME	**10–15 minutes**
MATERIALS	Three large pieces of paper or cardboard; magazines, catalogues, or supermarket handouts; scissors if your children can use them; glue.
PREPARATION	On each large piece of paper draw a picture to represent a topic. For example: a wardrobe (for clothes), a table with plates (for food), and a toy basket (for toys).

IN CLASS

1 Divide the children into three groups and give them a name (such as the Clothes Group, the Food Group, and the Toy Group).
2 Give each group some magazines, catalogues, or supermarket handouts.
3 Tell them that each group must tear (or cut) out pictures that correspond to their topic.
4 When they have torn out a fair number of pictures, give each group the large picture that corresponds to their topic and tell them to stick some of the pictures on to it.
5 Display their pictures on the wall.
6 Collect the pictures that are left over for the next lesson.

Lesson 2

TIME	**5–10 minutes**
MATERIALS	Pieces of card and pictures of objects from the three categories: enough for each group to have some from each category.
PREPARATION	Stick the pictures on to separate cards.

IN CLASS	1 Divide the class into groups.
	2 Give each group cards containing pictures from all three categories.
	3 Tell the children to separate the cards into Clothes, Food, and Toys. Go round helping them.

Lesson 3

TIME   **5–10 minutes**

PREPARATION   Prepare some worksheets like Worksheet 2.8 (page 156). You will need one for each child. It is a good idea to prepare extra tasks for children who work quickly.

IN CLASS
1 Draw some things on the board, for example: a snake, a ball, a tree, a kite, a house, a teddy bear.
2 Call one child out to the board and ask her/him to point to a toy.
3 When the child correctly points to a toy, give a lot of praise and draw a circle round the toy.
4 Repeat this procedure with two more children.
5 Indicate the three toys and say, *Toys.*
6 Draw six more things, three of which belong to the same category. For example: a cow, a book, an umbrella, a cat, a dog, and a car.
7 Call out a child, give her/him the chalk or board-pen, and tell her/him to draw a circle round all the animals. When she/he has done that successfully (perhaps with your help) give praise and let her/him clean the board.
8 Hand out the worksheets and tell the children to circle all the things to eat and go round to check if they are doing it correctly.
9 Hand out extra worksheets to those who finish quickly or let them colour in the drawings.

VARIATION   With younger children it is better to use real objects instead of pictures and do it as a whole-class activity. Ask them to bring you, for example, all the buttons they can find or all the rubbers, etc.

COMMENTS
1 After covering a number of topics, a classifying activity is a good way of consolidating vocabulary.
2 You can use the words from 'Class Monster' (1.5) if the children have already learnt them.

2.9 Recognition

AGE   4, 5, 6

TIME   **5–10 minutes**

AIMS   **Language:** to follow instructions, to practise vocabulary
Other: visual recognition

DESCRIPTION

The children select an object in a picture according to the teacher's instruction.

MATERIALS

Coloured pencils.

PREPARATION

Draw some objects on a sheet of paper as in Worksheet 2.9 (page 157). Make one copy for each child.

IN CLASS

1 Draw some animals on the board, for example: a snake, a sheep, a bird, a cat.

2 Tell the children *Now I'll draw a circle round the cat* (for example). Do so, slowly and clearly.

3 Call out one of the children, give her/him the chalk or board-pen, and tell her/him to draw a circle round the bird.

4 Then call out another child and tell her/him to draw a circle round the snake.

5 Give out the worksheets and tell the children to draw a circle round the fish.

6 When they have done this, ask them to colour it in. Continue for each item in turn.

VARIATION

With older children you can say, for example, *Colour the snake green*. When they have done that you can say *Colour the bird brown*, and so on.

2.10   Find the odd one out

AGE   4, 5, 6

TIME   5–10 minutes

AIMS   **Language:** to follow instructions, to practise vocabulary
                       Other: visual recognition, cognitive development

DESCRIPTION   The children have to recognize which item is different from the others.

PREPARATION   Prepare worksheets on the vocabulary you want to practise, as in Worksheet 2.10 (page 158).

IN CLASS   1 Draw four things on the board, one of which is very obviously different from the others: for example, three bananas and a dog.
                       2 Ask the children which thing is different. When they give you the answer, draw a circle round the odd one out.
                       3 Repeat stages 1 and 2 a few more times.
                       4 Hand out the worksheets and tell the children to draw a circle round the one that is different.
                       5 When you have checked their worksheets, they can colour in the picture they have circled.

VARIATION   With older children you can do this activity using shapes. For example: one circle and three triangles. This will reinforce the learning of shapes and develop pre-reading skills.

2.11   Spot the difference

AGE   4, 5, 6

TIME   5–10 minutes

AIMS   **Language:** to follow instructions, to practise vocabulary
                       Other: visual recognition

DESCRIPTION   The children try to find differences between two pictures.

PREPARATION   Prepare worksheets as in Worksheet 2.11 (page 159) and make
                       copies for all the children.

IN CLASS   1 Draw two pictures on the board. They should be broadly the
                          same, but with two or three obvious differences.

2 Ask the children if they can see any differences between the two
   pictures. If they find it difficult, you may need to help them.

   In picture A the girl is walking. In picture B she is running.
   In picture A it is sunny. In picture B it is raining.

3 When all the differences have been pointed out, hand out the
   worksheets and tell the children to see if they can find the
   differences.

4 When you have checked their work, they can colour the things
   that are different.

COMMENTS   As with the previous activity, the differences must be very obvious
                       and there must only be one or two.

3 All about me

This chapter concentrates on the children themselves and their immediate surroundings: family and likes and dislikes. It contains the most activities because small children are still largely egocentric. They learn to tell and ask each other their names and identify parts of the body. There is only a little on 'The family' because family situations are so diverse nowadays and we wished to avoid a stereotypical view. The best way to deal with this topic is to find out as much as you can about the family situation beforehand. You can let the children produce drawings or bring photos of the people who mean most to them and teach the appropriate vocabulary.

Food and toys are also of particular importance to children and work on these topics gives children the opportunity to talk about what they like and dislike, and learn to respect others' likes and dislikes. It also helps them to understand how things work and how they are made.

Songs and rhymes

3.1 What's your name?

AGE

All

TIME

10–15 minutes

AIMS

Language: asking and telling names
Other: confidence

MATERIALS

A toy or puppet.

IN CLASS

Lesson 1

1 When the children come in, introduce yourself and the puppet (in this case a dog).

Teacher: *Hello boys and girls. My name's …. This is Bingo.*

Walk up to a child and say as if Bingo was speaking:

Hello. What's your name? My name's Bingo.

2 Go round to each child doing the same. Encourage them to stroke the dog, which will help them relax. Don't force them to speak but if some try, praise their efforts saying: *Very good*. Don't forget to smile and nod, as at this stage the children need all the visual back-up and reassurance you can give them.

3 When you have finished this exercise, sing Bingo's song. You can pretend Bingo is singing.

What's your name?

I'm a little dog. My name is Bingo.
Bingo, Bingo. What's your name?
(S. M. Ward)

Sing it again and encourage the children to join in.

VARIATION

If you want to introduce other characters, toys, etc., you can add to the song. For example:

I'm a teddy bear. My name is Teddy.
Teddy, Teddy. What's your name?

This may be enough for one lesson.

Lesson 2

The next stage depends on the age of your pupils and how confident you think they are feeling. It could be done at a later stage in your course as revision.

4 Show the children your puppet and ask one child her or his name. Then teach them:

For a girl: *I'm a little girl. My name is Carla. Carla, Carla. What's your name?*

For a boy: *I'm a little boy. My name is Pedro. Pedro, Pedro. What's your name?*

5 If the children are confident, let them take the puppet and sing the song to each other.

FOLLOW-UP

In future, you can use the puppet to present new language. You can pretend to have a dialogue with the puppet. The children will soon want to take the part of the puppet.

COMMENTS

Having a familiar character which is integral in the learning process will give the children a sense of security and continuity. The main puppet can be a good character and you can introduce a naughty puppet who plays tricks on the good one. In time the children may make up spontaneous dialogues with the characters.

3.2 Where are you?

AGE	**All**
TIME	**5 minutes**
AIMS	**Language:** to ask where someone is and to respond; introductions; Total Physical Response
DESCRIPTION	The children sing a song and take turns at hiding.
MATERIALS	A puppet or cuddly toy.
IN CLASS	1 Give your puppet a name.

2 Sing the song, replacing 'Tommy Thumb' with the name of the puppet.

Tommy Thumb

Tom - my Thumb, Tom - my Thumb, Where are you?

Here I am, here I am, How do you do?

For example:

Billy, Billy, where are you?   *Hide the puppet behind your back*
Here I am, here I am.   *Bring the puppet from behind your back*

How do you do?   *Puppet shakes hands with one of the children*

(traditional)

Sing the song again and encourage the children to join in.

3 Now sing the song using the name of one of the children.

4 Get the child to stand when her/his name is mentioned.

5 Shake hands with her/him as you sing *How do you do?*

6 If the child is confident enough to continue, let her/him sing. You could let her/him hold the puppet or the toy.

7 Get one of the children to hide and then sing: *Hiroshi, Hiroshi, where are you?* The child appears and sings: *Here I am, Here I am.* Then you both sing: *How do you do?*

3.3   Birthday cake and song

AGE

All

TIME

Practice: 10 minutes **Party:** Variable

AIMS

Language: numbers, asking and telling age, birthday greetings
Other: awareness of celebrations, socializing

DESCRIPTION

The child who is celebrating her/his birthday puts 'candles' in a 'cake', and the others sing a birthday song. Then they have a class party.

MATERIALS

A big cardboard cake, cardboard candles, name cards, a bag, food and drink (if allowed).

PREPARATION

At the beginning of the school year make a big cardboard cake, candles, and a name card for each child. Cut some slots in the top of the cake, making sure they are the right size to fit the candles in. Find out from the parents/guardians or from the school how old each child is and when their birthday is.

IN CLASS

1 In the first class with the children stick the 'cake' on the wall low enough for the children to reach and tell them what it is. Show them the candles.

2 Ask a child: *How old are you?* Then supply the answer, holding up that number of fingers, and get the child to repeat: *I'm four.*

3 Take four candles and slot them in the 'cake'. Then take them out and let the child slot them in.

4 Repeat steps 3 and 4 with other children. If you have a very large class, you may have to limit the number but tell them they will all get a chance to do it on their birthday.

5 Teach them a birthday song, either the familiar 'Happy Birthday to You', which is in *Young Learners* by Sarah Phillips in this series, or this one:

Happy birthday once again

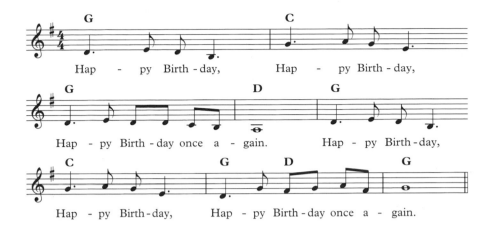

Happy Birthday, Happy Birthday,
Happy Birthday once again.
Happy Birthday, Happy Birthday,
Happy Birthday once again.
(S. M. Ward)

6 Whenever it is a child's birthday get them to put the right number of candles in the cake and stick their name card on the front of the cake. Everyone then sings a birthday song.

7 If it is allowed, you could have a little class party, perhaps enlisting the help of parents/guardians. This would give you a chance to practise functions such as Offering (*Would you like a ...?*), Accepting (*Yes, please.*), Refusing (*No, thanks.*), or Asking for (*Can I have a ...?*).

VARIATION

This song can be adapted to suit other celebrations, for example: Happy Easter, Happy Christmas, or Happy Name-day/Saint's day. (See Chapter 6, 'Festivals'.)

COMMENTS

1 Celebrating each child's birthday in class not only gives us an opportunity to revise certain language points—it also gives the birthday child a chance to feel important.

2 Small children will probably not know when their birthday is and some may be uncertain about their age. Therefore, you need to find out these facts before the school year begins.

3 Birthday conventions vary from country to country. Some may have cakes very different from the British idea of a birthday cake, and some may not celebrate birthdays at all. You could use whatever is meaningful to the children you teach, or if you want the children to learn about British/American etc. culture, you could make a birthday cake yourself or ask one of your friends or a parent to make one.

3.4   You've got me

AGE	**All**
TIME	**10–15 minutes**
AIMS	**Language:** parts of the body; Total Physical Response **Other:** physical co-ordination
DESCRIPTION	The children sing a song and do actions.
IN CLASS	1 Teach or revise the parts of the body by pointing to yourself and saying or eliciting the words. 2 Point to the parts of the body which come into the song and say them in order, encouraging the children to repeat them after you: *face, eyes, mouth, nose, body, legs, toes, hair.*

You've got me

On your face are some eyes,   *Point to the parts of the body*
a mouth and nose,
Ee-ai-ee-ai-o.

Then there's your body,   *Wiggle your body then touch your*
some legs, some toes,   *legs and then your toes.*
Ee-ai-ee-ai-o.

With some arms here and some hair there,	*Wave your arms and hold up some hair*
Here's some hair, there's some hair,	*Touch your eyebrows and eyelashes*
Everywhere there's hair, hair,	
Put them all together and you've got me,	*Bring the palms of your hands together and point them towards yourself*

Ee-ai-ee-ai-o.

(words V. Reilly; to the tune of 'Old MacDonald had a farm'—traditional)

3 Sing the song, encouraging the children to do the actions.

4 Sing the song again. By now some will be joining in the 'Ee-ai-ee-ai-o'.

5 Sing the song again, slowing it down in order to give the children time to supply the right word when you point to that part of the body.

3.5   If you're happy and you know it

AGE   **All**

TIME   **10–15 minutes**

AIMS   **Language:** to talk about feelings; Total Physical Response

DESCRIPTION   The children sing a song and do the actions.

PREPARATION   Prepare the flashcards as on page 57.

IN CLASS

1 Show the flashcard for *happy* and teach them the word. Do the same for *sad* and *angry*. You can also mime appropriate facial expressions.

2 Ask: *How do you feel today? Happy? Sad? Angry?* Then go round asking each child and showing the appropriate card.

3 Hold up the 'Happy' card and elicit the word.

If you're happy and you know it

hap - py and you know it, clap your hands, (*clap*, *clap*) If you're

hap - py and you know it, then your face is going to show it. If you're

If you're happy and you know it, clap your hands,	*clap, clap*
If you're happy and you know it, clap your hands,	*clap, clap*
If you're happy and you know it, then your face is going to show it,	*big smile*
If you're happy and you know it, clap your hands.	*clap, clap*
If you're sad and you know it, wipe your eyes,	*sniff, sniff*
If you're sad and you know it, wipe your eyes,	*sniff, sniff*
If you're sad and you know it, then your face is going to show it,	*sad face*
If you're sad and you know it, wipe your eyes.	*sniff, sniff*
If you're angry and you know it, stamp your feet,	*stamp, stamp*
If you're angry and you know it, stamp your feet,	*stamp, stamp*
If you're angry and you know it, then your face is going to show it,	*frown*
If you're angry and you know it, stamp your feet.	*stamp, stamp*

(traditional)

4 Sing the first verse, with a very happy face. Clap your hands at the right time.

5 Sing the first verse again, getting the children to join in with the clapping.

6 Then show the 'Sad' card and elicit the word. Put on a very sad expression, start sniffing loudly and wiping your eyes, and sing the second verse.

7 Sing the second verse again, encouraging the children to mime the crying.

8 Show the 'Angry' card and elicit the word. Put on a very angry expression and sing the third verse, stamping your feet at the right time.

9 Sing the verse again and encourage the children to join in the stamping. (They won't need much encouragement!)

10 Sing the song all the way through.

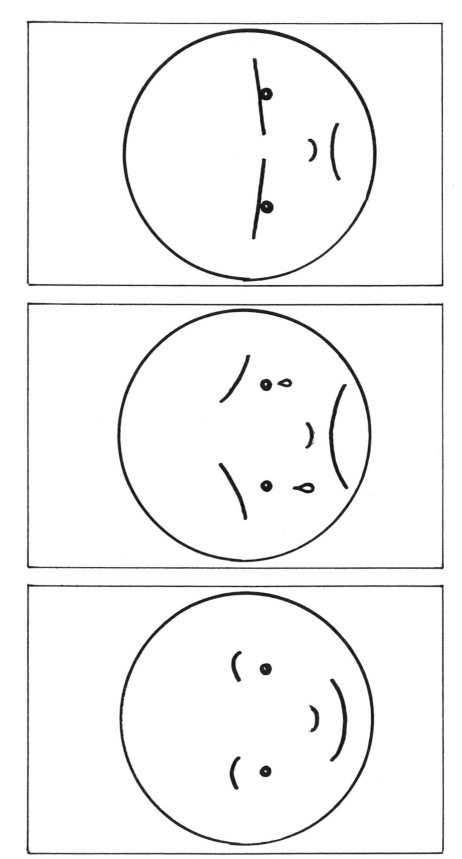

FOLLOW-UP

Ask the children how they feel at the start of each class. You could make a poster with *Today we feel …* and get one of the children to choose the correct flashcard and stick it on the poster.

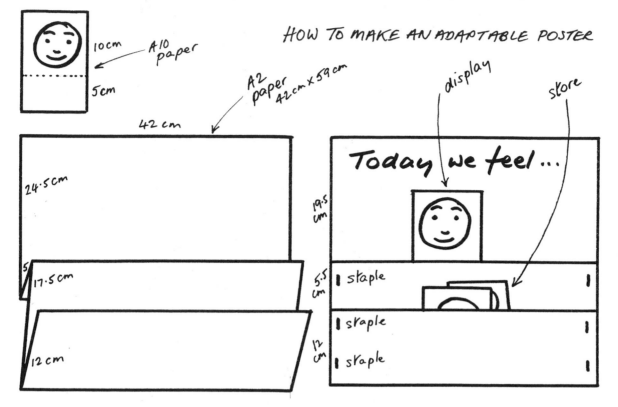

COMMENTS

1 You may find that very young children will not even try to sing, but they will enjoy the actions and they are listening to you.

2 This song is on the *Jingle Bells* cassette.

3.6   My favourite toys

AGE

All

TIME

15 minutes

AIMS

Language: toy vocabulary, *I love …*
Other: looking at catalogues and choosing

DESCRIPTION

The children choose their favourite toy and sing a song.

MATERIALS

Pictures or catalogues of toys (most toy companies and stores are only too willing to part with them) or real toys.

PREPARATION

If you have no real toys, cut some pictures of toys from magazines or catalogues and stick them on pieces of card. Make sure you have a picture of a teddy bear, a ball, and a xylophone for yourself.

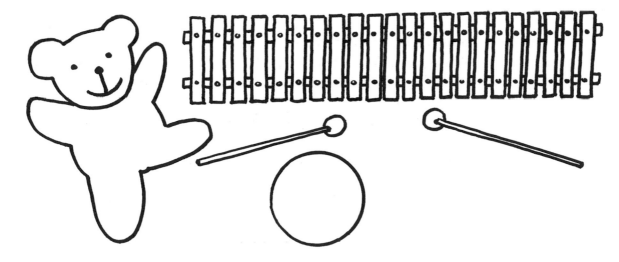

IN CLASS

1 Let the children sit on the floor and tell them to choose a picture of their favourite toy or the real thing. There may be some squabbles but you can tell them that two people can like the same thing. If two or more choose the same toy, they can sit together.

2 When they have all chosen their favourite toy, tell them the words for the things. You could say, for example: *Carmen's got a dinosaur and Ali's got a police car.*

3 When you have told them the names for their toys, show them a picture of a teddy bear, a ball, and a xylophone and say: *These are my favourite toys.*

These are my favourite toys

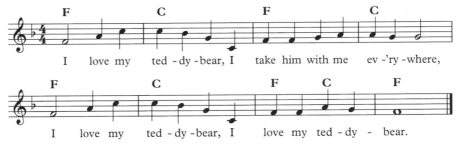

I love my teddy bear,
I take him with me everywhere,
I love my teddy bear,
I love my teddy bear.

I love my bouncing ball,
I bounce it on the floor, I bounce it on the wall,
I love my bouncing ball,
I love my bouncing ball.

I love my xylophone,
Bing bong bing bong bing bong bong,
I love my xylophone,
I love my xylophone.

(S. M. Ward)

4 Show the picture of the teddy bear and make a hugging gesture. Sing the first verse of the song.

5 Show the picture of the ball and make a hugging gesture. Sing the second verse, miming bouncing the ball at the appropriate moment.

6 Show the picture of the xylophone and sing the third verse, miming playing the xylophone.

7 Repeat the song, encouraging the children to join in with the actions and words.

8 (Optional) If possible, make up more verses for the song with the children's favourite toys.

3.7   I am a robot man

AGE   **All**

TIME   **10 minutes**

AIMS   **Language:** to practise *can* for ability, and the verbs *sit, stand, shake hands*; Total Physical Response

DESCRIPTION   The children sing a song and do the actions.

IN CLASS   1 Make your arms and legs stiff and walk about like a robot. Say: *I'm a robot.*

2 Sit down stiffly on a chair and say: *I can sit.*

3 Stand up stiffly and say: *I can stand.*

4 Walk over to a child and shake hands with him/her saying: *I can shake hands.*

5 Go through steps 1–4 again, getting the children to copy you.

6 Sing the song several times, doing the actions and encouraging the children to join in.

I am a robot man

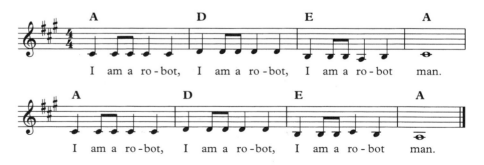

I am a ro - bot, I am a ro - bot, I am a ro - bot man.

I am a ro - bot, I am a ro - bot, I am a ro - bot man.

Chorus
I am a robot, I am a robot,
I am a robot man.
I am a robot, I am a robot,
I am a robot man.

I can sit and I can stand,
I am a robot man.
I can shake you by the hand,
I am a robot man.

(S. M. Ward)

COMMENTS

The children will enjoy it much more if you put on a metallic, robot-like voice.

FOLLOW-UP

If time permits or in another lesson you can play 'Robot Game' (see 3.18). Children can also make robots out of junk materials (old boxes etc.) as in 'Make a robot' (3.27).

3.8 Five currant buns

AGE

All

TIME

10 minutes

AIMS

Language: to practise numbers and food vocabulary, to express likes and dislikes; Total Physical Response

DESCRIPTION

The children sing a song and act it out.

MATERIALS

Five real buns or a picture with five buns on. (They are made of a sweet dough with dried fruit inside—see 6.13, 'Hot Cross Buns', page 149, for a recipe.)

IN CLASS

1 Show the children the buns. Tell them that they are currant buns with sugar on the top. Count them, encouraging the children to join in.

2 Sing or play the song to the children, pointing to the buns.

Five currant buns

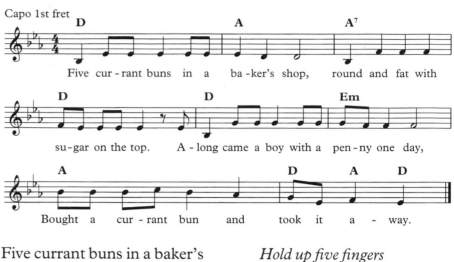

Five currant buns in a baker's shop,	*Hold up five fingers*
Round and fat with sugar on the top	*Make large, circular actions with your hand and pat your head*
Along came a boy with a penny one day,	*Pretend to hold a penny in your hand*
Bought a currant bun and took it away.	*Slap your right hand down on your left hand and pretend that your right hand is pulling your left hand away*

(traditional)

3 Call out five children to be the currant buns.

4 Sing: *Five currant buns in a baker's shop,* indicating the five children.

5 Sing: *Round and fat,* miming this, *with sugar on the top.* Pat each child gently on the head.

6 Sing: *In came* (put your own name here) *with a penny one day, Bought a currant bun …* Slap your palm down gently on the palm of the first child to mime paying.

7 Sing *… and took it away.* Lead the child away.

8 Sing *Four currant buns in a baker's shop* etc. and lead the second child away.

9 Sing *Three currant buns in a baker's shop* etc. and lead the third child away.

10 Sing *Two currant buns in a baker's shop* etc. and lead the fourth child away.

11 Sing *One currant bun in a baker's shop* etc. and lead the last child away.

12 Call out five more 'buns' and five 'shoppers'. This time let the children go through the routine while you and the others are

singing. Put the name of each 'shopper' into the song when it is her/his turn to buy a bun.

13 If you are using real buns, cut them up and give each child a piece. Get them to say: *I like it* or *I don't like it*. If you have not got any real buns, you could use food that is available in the country where you teach.

FOLLOW-UP   The children could play at shops, practising: *Can I have a currant bun, please? That's … pence, please.*

COMMENTS   This song is on the *Super Songs* cassette.

3.9 The wheels on the bus

AGE   **All**

TIME   **5–10 minutes**

AIMS   **Language:** vocabulary about transport and families; Total Physical Response

DESCRIPTION   The children sing a song and mime the actions.

MATERIALS   A toy bus or model of a bus (not essential).

PREPARATION   If you have no toy bus, you could make the model bus on Worksheet 3.9. See also the flashcard on page 184.

IN CLASS   1 Show the children the bus, tell them what it is, and ask if they have ever been in one. Turn the wheels and say: *The wheels on the bus go round and round.*
2 Teach or revise the words *mummy*, *daddy*, *children*, and *baby*.
3 Sit down on a chair and sing the song, doing the actions.

The wheels on the bus

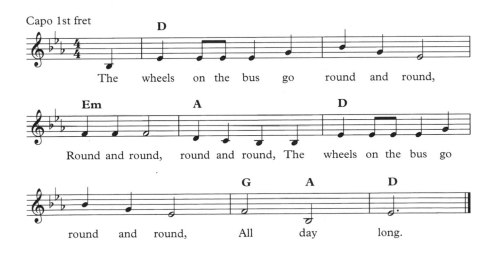

The wheels on the bus go round and round, Round and round, round and round, The wheels on the bus go round and round, All day long.	*Make circling movements with your arms*
The children on the bus go wriggle wriggle wriggle, wriggle wriggle wriggle, wriggle wriggle wriggle, The children on the bus go wriggle wriggle wriggle, All day long.	*Wriggle*
The mummies on the bus go 'Don't do that, Don't do that, Don't do that, Don't do that.' The mummies on the bus go 'Don't do that.' All day long	*Wag your finger*
The daddies on the bus go read read read, Read read read, read read read, The daddies on the bus go read read read All day long.	*Pretend to read a newspaper (arms open wide)*
The babies on the bus go 'wah wah wah, wah wah wah, wah wah wah,' The babies on the bus go 'wah wah wah.' All day long.	*Pretend to cry*

(traditional, adapted)

4 Repeat the song, and get the children to join in the actions.

5 If your classroom has chairs that you can move, you can put them in two rows one behind the other like the seats on a bus and the children can sit on them. Some children can be the children, others can be the mummies, the daddies, and the babies.

FOLLOW-UP

The children can make the bus in 3.26.

COMMENTS

This song is on the *Super Songs* cassette.

3.10   Here we go looby loo

AGE

All

TIME

10–15 minutes

AIMS

Language: body vocabulary, following instructions; Total Physical Response
Other: *left* and *right*

DESCRIPTION

The children sing, dance, and follow instructions in a song.

IN CLASS

1 Revise the parts of the body. Teach the concept of left and right by turning your back to the children, waving your right hand in

the air and saying: *right hand*. Put that hand down and then wave your left hand in the air and say: *left hand*. Do the same with your right foot and your left foot. You can even turn it into a little chant.

2 The children get into a circle.

3 At first you sing or play the song and the children just follow the actions.

Here we go looby loo

(Chorus)

Here we go looby loo,
Here we go looby light,
Here we go looby loo,
All on a Saturday night.

Form a circle and walk round holding hands

Put your right hand in,
Put your right hand out,
Shake it a little, a little,
And turn yourself about.

*Stop walking round,
Stand in a circle and do the actions*

(Chorus)

Put your left hand in,
Put your left hand out,
Shake it a little, a little,
And turn yourself about.

Form a circle and walk round holding hands

Do the actions

(Chorus)

Put your right foot in,
Put your right foot out,
Shake it a little, a little,
And turn yourself about.

(Chorus)

Put your left foot in,
Put your left foot out,
Shake it a little, a little,
And turn yourself about.

(Chorus)

Put your whole self in,
Put your whole self out,
Shake it a little, a little,
And turn yourself about.

(traditional)

4 Repeat the song if the children like it and encourage them to join in.

COMMENTS

1 Do not worry if the children get their right and left mixed up. Some children take a long time to learn this concept and there are even adults who still have difficulty with it.

2 This song is on the *Super Songs* cassette.

3.11 I've got a lot of pets

AGE

All

TIME

10–15 minutes

AIMS

Language: animal vocabulary, *I've got...*, *I like...*; Total Physical Response

DESCRIPTION

The children learn the names of animals, mime them, and sing a song.

MATERIALS

Pictures of the animals in the song (see the Flashcards on pages 177–8).

PREPARATION

Prepare the pictures.

IN CLASS

1 Ask the children if they have got any pets at home. If not, ask them which pet they would like to have.

2 Show the animal pictures one at a time and teach the names. Stick them on the board in the order of the song.

3 Let some of the children pretend to be animals. The others try to guess what they are.

4 Sing the song, pointing to each animal as it is mentioned.

I've got a lot of pets

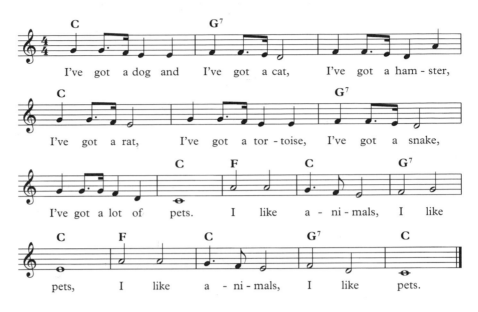

I've got a dog and I've got a cat,
I've got a hamster, I've got a rat,
I've got a tortoise, I've got a snake,
I've got a lot of pets.

I like animals, I like pets,
I like animals, I like pets.

I've got a rabbit, I've got a mouse,
I've got a parrot in my house,
I've got a monkey, I've got a horse,
I've got a lot of pets.

I like animals, I like pets,
I like animals, I like pets.

(S. M. Ward)

5 Get the children to repeat the song after you line by line and then sing it through.

6 Sing the song again. One of the children might like to point to the animals as they are mentioned.

7 The children could make suggestions and add other pets to the song.

FOLLOW-UP

If you have more than fifteen minutes with the children, they could do some free painting or drawing. Each one draws their pet or the one they would like to have.

3.12 Body Rhymes

AGE	**All**
TIME	**5 minutes each**
AIMS	**Language:** parts of the body; Total Physical Response
DESCRIPTION	The children say rhymes, doing the actions.

IN CLASS

1 Say the rhyme all the way through, doing exaggerated actions.
2 Get the children to join in with the actions as you repeat the rhyme.
3 Encourage the children to join in with the rhyme when they seem confident enough.

Two little eyes

Two little eyes to look around	*Point to your eyes and look from side to side*
Two little ears to hear each sound	*Cup your hands behind your ears*
One little nose to smell what's sweet	*Point to your nose and lift your head*
One little mouth that likes to eat	*Point to your mouth and pretend to eat*

(traditional)

Two clean hands

Two clean hands and two fat thumbs	*Hold out your hands, then stick your thumbs up*
Eight little fingers,	*Tuck your thumb behind your fingers and wriggle your fingers*
Ten little toes,	*Hold up both hands wriggling all your fingers and quickly point to your feet*
One round head goes nod, nod, nodding,	*Draw a circle in front of your face with your index finger, then nod your head*
Two eyes peeping,	*Shade your eyes with your hand and then peep out from under it*
One tiny nose.	*Point to your nose*

(traditional)

COMMENTS	These rhymes are on the *Super Songs* cassette.

3.13   Jelly on a plate

AGE	**All**
TIME	**5 minutes each**
AIMS	**Language:** to practise food vocabulary, likes/dislikes; stress and rhythm; Total Physical Response
DESCRIPTION	The children say a rhyme and then act it out.
MATERIALS	Flashcards of jelly, sausages, and any other food that you want to include (see page 186).

IN CLASS

1   Teach or practise the food items by holding up the flashcard and drilling the word.
2   Teach this rhyme a line at a time.

Jelly on a Plate

●   ●   ●   ●
Jelly on a plate, jelly on a plate
        ●   ●
Wibble wobble, wibble wobble
   ●   ●
Jelly on a plate.
   ●   ●   ●   ●
Sausages in a pan, sausages in a pan
   ●   ●
Turn them over, turn them over,
   ●   ●
Sausages in a pan.
(traditional)

3   When the children can say the rhyme quite well, call out five children to stand at the front of the class to be jellies. While the others are saying the rhyme, the five 'jellies' shake themselves about.
4   Then call out five 'sausages'. Get them to lie down on the floor for the second verse. When it comes to *Turn them over*, the children roll over on the floor. If it is not possible to lie on the floor, the 'sausages' can just stand up and turn around.
5   Repeat this with other groups of children.

VARIATION

This rhyme can easily be adapted to suit local foods in different countries. For example:
Chapatti in a pan, Tortilla in a pan, Croissants in the oven.

COMMENTS

1   The amount of children you have out at a time really depends on you and the size of your class.
2   This rhyme is on the *Super Songs* cassette.

3.14   Pat-a-cake, pat-a-cake

AGE	**All**
TIME	**5–10 minutes**
AIMS	**Language:** vocabulary, pronunciation of /p/ and /b/, stress and rhythm **Other:** hand and rhythm co-ordination
DESCRIPTION	The children recite a rhyme and clap on the stressed words.
IN CLASS	1 Say the rhyme, clapping on the stressed syllables. Encourage the children to join in with the clapping to mark the rhythm. 2 Teach the rhyme line by line (don't forget the clapping).

Pat-a-cake, pat-a-cake

Pat-a-cake, pat-a-cake, baker's man,

Bake me a cake, as fast as you can,

Prick it and pat it and mark it with 'B',

And put it in the oven, for baby and me.

For baby and me, for baby and me

Put it in the oven, for baby and me

(traditional)

3 When you have said it a few times, put in the children's names and initials. For example:

… mark it with C, and put it in the oven for Carlos and me.

COMMENTS

This song is on the *Super Songs* cassette. Another song you could use is 'Clap your hands', which is also on the cassette.

3.15 I like toys

AGE

All

TIME

10–15 minutes

AIMS

Language: toy vocabulary, stress and rhythm, likes/dislikes
Other: hand co-ordination

DESCRIPTION

The children chant and clap the rhythm.

MATERIALS

Flashcards of the toys in the chant (see pages 184 and 185).

IN CLASS

1 Draw a smiley face on the board and say *I like* … . Get the children to repeat it.

2 Hold up one of the flashcards and say: *I like* …, inserting the word. The children need to repeat what you say. Go through the same procedure for some of the other cards.
3 Draw another smiley face except with the smile from ear to ear and say *I love* … and go through the procedure for *I like* … with the remaining flashcards.
4 Say the chant, clapping on the stressed words or syllables. The children should learn it as a whole, not line by line.
5 Ask the children to suggest other toys to include in the chant.

I like toys

● ●
I like toys

● ●
Dolls, cars, trains

● ●
I love them all

● ●
Puppets and games
(V. Reilly)

FOLLOW-UP

Free painting. The children paint or draw their favourite toy.

Games

3.16 Step forward

AGE	5, 6
TIME	**5–10 minutes**
AIMS	**Language:** to practise *have got*, to revise the names for members of the family, listening **Other:** following the rules of a game
MATERIALS	Chalk or string.
DESCRIPTION	The children listen to instructions to hear which are relevant to them.

PREPARATION

1 Prepare instructions according to what language you wish to practise and the level of your learners.
2 Draw a line across the classroom halfway between the two side walls. If you cannot draw on the floor you could use a long piece of string.

IN CLASS

1 The children line up with their backs to one wall. Demonstrate what they should do (explaining in their first language if necessary), then stand with your back against the opposite wall.
2 Say, for example: *Step forward if you have got a Maria in your family.*
3 Any child who has got someone of that name in their family must step forward and say, for example: *My mother's name is Maria.*
4 The game continues with you giving different names.
5 The first child to cross the line is the winner and can take your place for the next round. Stop playing before the children get bored.

VARIATION 1

With shy or younger children you can leave out step 3.

VARIATION 2

You can use other actions and target language, for example, *Stand up if you're wearing green.*

3.17 Change places

AGE	5, 6
TIME	10–15 minutes
AIMS	Various depending on what you want to practise
DESCRIPTION	The children change places according to the instructions given by the leader.
PREPARATION	Put chairs in a circle: enough for every child.
IN CLASS	1 You are the leader. Stand in the middle whilst the children sit on the chairs around you.
	2 Say for example: *Change places if you are wearing green.* All those wearing green must change places. At the same time you try and sit down on one of the chairs.
	3 The child left standing is the leader and must say: *Change places if you are wearing …*
COMMENTS	This game can be used to practise other language, for example, *Change places if you've got a sister. Change places if you like chocolate.*

3.18 Robot game

AGE	**All**
TIME	**10 minutes**
AIMS	**Language:** listening, giving/following instructions, Total Physical Response
	Other: encouraging politeness
DESCRIPTION	The children listen to instructions and obey only when the speaker says *Please.*
IN CLASS	1 Call out one of the children and tell her/him that she/he is a robot and must follow your instructions.
	2 Say things like: *Sit down please. Stand up please. Walk to the door, please.* The child must do what you tell them to do.
	3 Choose two children to demonstrate. One is the robot and the other gives instructions. Make sure they say *Please.*
	4 Put all the children into pairs and get them to practise being robots and giving instructions.
	5 Tell the children to sit down and explain that you are going to play a game. You give the instructions but the children only obey if you say *Please* (see 2.7, 'Simon says').

VARIATION

If the children do not have enough language to give instructions, you can leave out steps 3 and 4.

COMMENTS

1 Normally anyone who carries out the instruction when you do not say *Please* is out of the game, but you need to be more lenient with younger children.
2 See also 3.7, 'I am a robot man' and 3.27, 'Make a robot'.

3.19   The gingerbread man game

AGE

5–6

TIME

15–20 minutes

AIMS

Language: reading and saying numbers, parts of the body
Other: to practise hand control

DESCRIPTION

The children colour and cut out a 'gingerbread man' and play a game.

MATERIALS

A copy of Worksheet 3.19 for every child (see page 160), scissors, a dice (one between 4–5 children), brown pencils or crayons.

DESCRIPTION

If you have children who cannot use scissors you will have to cut out the 'gingerbread man' beforehand or perforate the outline with a sewing-machine.

IN CLASS

1 Give each child a 'gingerbread man' and tell them what it is.
2 Tell them to colour him brown.
3 Tell the children to cut round him. (They may need some help with this.)
4 Revise the parts of the body, pointing to yourself or a child. Ask the children which numbers correspond to which parts of the gingerbread man's body, for example, *What number is his head?* Try and elicit the number from the children.
5 The children then cut along the lines so that he is in six parts.
6 In groups of four or five, the children place all the parts of their 'gingerbread man' in the middle.
7 Explain that the object of the game is to retrieve their 'man'.
8 The first child throws the dice and says, for example, *six—his body*.
9 The next child follows the same procedure.
10 If they throw a number they already have, they miss a turn. If they do not say the number and then the part of the body they cannot take the part of the body.

COMMENTS

This activity can be used as a follow-up to 'The gingerbread man' story (3.20) or making gingerbread men biscuits (3.28). The children can also make a 'gingerbread man' puppet (3.29).

VARIATION

Instead of a 'gingerbread man' you can use a snowman, a bear, etc.

Stories

3.20 The gingerbread man

AGE	5, 6
TIME	**5–10 minutes**
AIMS	**Language:** verbs such as *walk*, *hop*, etc., listening, Total Physical Response **Other:** eye–hand co-ordination, following a story, to experience food from a different culture
DESCRIPTION	The children listen to a story.
MATERIALS	Gingerbread biscuit mixture (if possible), 'gingerbread man' puppet (see 3.29), pictures of the animals in the story.
PREPARATION	1 Make gingerbread men biscuits as in 3.28 and 'gingerbread man' puppets as in 3.29. 2 Read the story in advance and practise telling it.

The gingerbread man

One day an old woman was making some gingerbread.'

Mime kneading.

She decided to make a gingerbread man.

Tell the children to put their puppets on their fingers.

She made a gingerbread man with currants for his eyes and mouth and sweets for his buttons. Then she put him in the oven.

Mime putting him in the oven.
Fan yourself as you 'open the door' to show it is hot.

When he was ready she opened the door and looked inside.

Mime what you are saying.

The gingerbread man jumped out of the oven, and ran out of the house and down the road.

Using your puppet, mime what he did.

He shouted to the old woman: 'Run, run as fast as you can. You can't catch me, I'm the gingerbread man.'

Try to get the children to repeat the repeat the gingerbread man's words.

The old woman and her cat ran after the gingerbread man but they could not catch him.

Point to the cat on the blackboard.
Mime the old woman running, and then shake your head and mime the action of catching someone.

The gingerbread man ran and ran and he came to a cow.

Mime using the puppet.
Point to the cow picture on the blackboard.

The cow said, 'Stop. I want to eat you.'
The old woman, the cat, and the cow ran after the gingerbread man but they could not catch him.

Push the flat of your hand towards the children as a gesture for 'Stop'.

The gingerbread man said, 'I've run away from the old woman and her cat and I can run away from you too.
Run, run as fast as you can. You can't catch me, I'm the gingerbread man.'

Get the children to repeat 'Run, run, 'as fast as you can' etc.

Soon the gingerbread man saw a horse. 'Stop,' said the horse. 'I want to eat you.' The gingerbread man just laughed and ran faster. The old woman, the …, the …, and the … all ran after him down the road.

Make the puppet run.
Point to the pictures and try and elicit the animals—cat, cow, and horse.

He said, 'I've run away from the old woman, the …, and the …, and I can run away from you too.'

Point to the pictures and elicit the words—cat and cow.

'Run, run as fast as you can. You can't catch me, I'm the gingerbread man.'

Hopefully the children should now be muttering the words on their own, although they will be too shy to say them out loud without you eliciting them.

After a few minutes the gingerbread man saw a goat. 'Stop,' said the goat. 'I want to eat you.' The gingerbread man laughed and said, 'I've run away from the old woman, the …, the …, and the …, and I can run away you too.'
The old woman, the …, the …, the …, and the … ran tafter him but they could not catch him.

Point to the pictures and elicit the words.
Point to all the pictures as the children say them.

He ran and ran down the road shouting.

Move the puppet.
Try and elicit the gingerbread man's words: 'Run, run, as fast as you can, you can't catch me, I'm the gingerbread man'.

After some time the gingerbread man saw a fox standing by a tree. Before the fox could say anything the gingerbread man said, 'I've run away from the old woman, the cat, the cow, the horse, and the goat, and I can run away from you.' The fox laughed and said, 'I don't want to eat you.'

Shake your head and make an eating gesture.

The gingerbread man stopped running. The fox said, 'I want to be your friend. Let's walk together.' So they walked along together.

Make the puppet walk.

They came to a river.

Make a 'wave' action with your hand.

The fox said, 'Jump on to my back and I'll carry you across.'

Do the actions with the puppet.

The gingerbread man jumped on to the fox's back but the water started to get deeper.

Do the actions with the puppet.

'Jump on to my shoulders,' said the fox.
The gingerbread man jumped on to the fox's shoulders.

Point to your shoulders.
Make the puppet jump on to your shoulder.

But the water got deeper and deeper and the fox said 'Jump on to my head.'

Point to your head.

The gingerbread man jumped on to the fox's head.	*Make the puppet jump on to your head.*
SNAP! went the fox's mouth.	*With your free hand close your fingers like a mouth.*
And that was the end of the gingerbread man.	*Make the gingerbread man disappear behind your back.*

IN CLASS

1 Give the children their gingerbread men to eat, reminding them what they are called.
2 Then they make 'gingerbread man' puppets (see 3.29) so that they can use them whilst you are telling the story.
3 Using your puppet, show the children that he can walk, jump, hop, dance, and run.
4 Call out *run*, *hop*, etc. Encourage the children to make their puppets do the actions.
5 Ask the children who the puppet is.
6 Show them the pictures of the animals in the story and try and elicit the English names.
7 Stick the pictures on the blackboard or wall in the following order: cat, cow, horse, goat, fox.
8 Tell the story, moving your gingerbread man puppet and pointing to the animals.

FOLLOW-UP 1

Play the 'gingerbread man' game (3.19).

FOLLOW-UP 2

In another lesson tell the story again, eliciting as many words as possible. Then get the children to act it out.

3.21 Spot's birthday: the book

AGE

All

TIME

10–15 minutes

AIMS

Language: listening, animal vocabulary, *Where is …?*, numbers
Other: introduction to books, deducing from clues, drama

DESCRIPTION

The teacher reads a story to the children, who act it out.

MATERIALS

The book *Spot's Birthday* by E. Hill, a picture or model of a birthday cake with candles (see 3.3); pictures of the following animals: a dog, a lion, a hippo, a bear, a penguin, a monkey, a crocodile, and a tortoise.

IN CLASS

1 Revise or teach the words for the different animals.
2 If possible, get the children to sit on a mat round your chair.

3 Show the picture of the birthday cake and ask the children if they know what it is and when we eat it. Point to the candles and count them encouraging the children to join in with you.

4 Show the children the book. Point to Spot and say: *This is Spot. He's a dog.* Then point to Spot and the birthday cake and say: *It's Spot's birthday today* (translate if necessary).

5 Open the book at the first page, point to the big dog and say: *This is Spot's mummy.* Point to the balloons and say: *Spot's having a party.*

6 Point to Spot with his eyes closed and say: *Spot's playing a game of hide-and-seek with his friends.* (The children may know the name for this game in their own language. If they do, you could elicit it.)

7 Say: *Where are Spot's friends?* Go through the pages, encouraging the children to guess which animal is hidden in each place. Then lift the flaps to show them and tell them the character's name.

8 Ask for ten volunteers to act out the story and call them to the front of the class. Give them roles according to the characters in the book.

9 Tell 'Spot' to close her/his eyes and count to ten (with your help). Tell the others to hide under the desks, behind the curtains, in cupboards, etc.

10 When 'Spot' has finished counting, get her/him to say: *Ready or not, here I come.* She/he then has to try to find the other characters.

COMMENTS

You may find that the youngest children will not sit still while they are not involved, so you can let them all hide. It does not matter if they are not well concealed. Like Leo the lion, a lot of very young children think that if they can't see you, you can't see them.

VARIATION 1

Another useful book on the theme of birthdays is *My Presents* by Rod Campbell (see Further Reading). It also consists of surprises hidden behind flaps and could be exploited in a similar way.

VARIATION 2

You might like to make your own flap book on the theme of birthdays or 'hide and seek'.

1 Get the children to draw different animals on sheets of paper.

2 Cover each animal with a picture of a different place in a house: a curtain, a bed, a fridge, etc. Stick the picture down with sticky tape along one edge only.

3 Staple or sew the pages together.

This idea can be adapted to different topics, such as: 'Where are the animals on the farm?' 'Where are the children at the seaside?' 'What food is in different containers?'

You can then read the class their own story, which gives a great sense of achievement.

3.22   Spot's birthday: the video

AGE

All

TIME

10 minutes

AIMS

Language: animal vocabulary, *Where's/Where are …?*, *Who's …?*, numbers

Other: deducing from clues, drama

DESCRIPTION

The children watch a video and try to guess who the different animals are.

MATERIALS

The video *Children's TV Favourites Volume 2*, pictures of a lion, a hippo, a bear, a penguin, a crocodile, a tortoise and a dog, a picture of a birthday cake.

PREPARATION

Watch the video before the lesson and make sure you know when to stop it.

IN CLASS

1   Revise or teach the animal vocabulary.
2   Show the cake and ask the children if they know what it is. Point to the candles and count them, encouraging the children to join in.
3   Start the video and pause it on the frame of Spot and his mother. Point to Spot and say: *It's Spot's birthday today.* Point to Spot's mother and say: *This is Spot's mummy.*
4   Continue showing the video, pausing it just before interesting scenes, and ask questions as in 3.21. Encourage the children to join in while Spot is counting up to ten and when his friends sing 'Happy birthday to you'.
5   Show the whole video again without stopping it.
6   Play 'hide and seek' as in 3.21.

Art and craft activities

3.23 Faces—an information gap activity

AGE

4, 5, 6

TIME

10–15 minutes

AIMS

Language: to revise the parts of the face; to let the children give some instructions; listening to each other

Other: eye–hand co-ordination, colour recognition

DESCRIPTION

The children paint features on a paper plate 'face', following instructions given by their partners.

MATERIALS

A screen (an old sheet and some pegs), paints or crayons, paper plates or cardboard circles, face pictures (see Preparation).

PREPARATION

Draw some pictures of faces and colour each one differently (or the children could do this in a previous lesson). Put up the screen so that it is ready for the activity.

MATERIALS

1 Practise the colours and the parts of the face, and the question *What colour is …?*

2 Divide the class into pairs.

3 Put one child from each pair on one side of the screen with the paints and paper plate, and the other child on the other side with the picture.

4 The child with the paints asks, for example, *What colour is the nose?* When the other child replies, for example, *Yellow*, the first child paints a yellow nose on the paper plate, and so on until the face is complete.

COMMENTS

1 Do not be too strict about the children's language as long as it is English. The object is for them to communicate with the language resources they have, for example: *Nose—what colour? Nose—yellow.*

2 If it is difficult for you to rig up a screen, the children could simply sit on chairs back to back.

3 If you have a large class, you may find it necessary to give some of the children a quiet activity to do while you are involved with those who are doing the face-painting, or spread it over several lessons.

3.24   **Pizza faces**

AGE	4, 5, 6
TIME	**20 minutes**
AIMS	**Language:** food vocabulary, parts of the face, understanding instructions
	Other: preparing food, exploring creative possibilities with food, task-based learning
DESCRIPTION	The children create faces with food materials.
MATERIALS	Some hamburger buns (half of one for each child), and ingredients to make the 'faces', for example: tomato sauce (skin), chorizo/pepperoni/sausage (eyes), slices of fresh tomato (nose), slices of red pepper (mouth), slices of green pepper (eyebrows), slices of mushroom (ears), grated cheese (hair/beard).
	These ingredients are merely a suggestion—what you actually use depends on what is available or in season.
PREPARATION	Prepare all the ingredients and place them in bowls. It is advisable to have several bowls of each type of food in case some children cannot reach. Put the halved buns on separate pieces of tin foil for the children to work on.

IN CLASS

1 Teach the children the parts of the face (away from the food if possible).
2 Show them the food ingredients.
3 Elicit the word *skin*, show them the tomato sauce, and tell them the English word. Put some on a bun.
4 Continue to do this for the whole 'face', making the pizza as you go.
5 Let the children make their pizzas. The children could say what they are doing as you go round monitoring.

6 You can cook the pizzas for a class snack if you have the facilities, or you could wrap them in the foil for the children to cook at home.

VARIATION

If cooking is a problem in your school then you could stick pictures of food on to paper plates (the pizza base). On Worksheet 3.24 (page 161) there are some drawings of the food so that you can photocopy them and cut them out, ready for the children to colour and stick.

3.25   My family

AGE	**All**
TIME	**15 minutes**
AIMS	**Language:** family vocabulary **Other:** drawing
DESCRIPTION	The children draw pictures of their families and talk about them.
MATERIALS	Paper, coloured pencils or crayons, a photo of your family (optional)

IN CLASS

1 Show the children a photo of your family if you have one, or draw a simple picture on the board. Point to the people and talk about them: *This is my mummy. This is my sister. Her name's … . This is my baby. This is me.*

2 Ask the children to draw pictures of their families.

3 As they draw, go round talking to the children individually about them in English. (Be sensitive to different family circumstances.) Encourage the children to point to their family members and say who they are in English.

4 Display the pictures on the wall. Point to some of the people and talk about them: *This is Mima's brother. Who's this?* Encourage the children to join in.

FOLLOW-UP   Encourage the children to bring in photos of their families and talk about them.

3.26   Make a bus

AGE	4, 5, 6
TIME	**15–20 minutes**
AIMS	**Language:** to understand instructions, to revise *bus* and family vocabulary **Other:** eye–hand co-ordination
DESCRIPTION	The children make a model bus following instructions.
MATERIALS	Photocopies of Worksheet 3.26 (see page 162), coloured pens/pencils/crayons, scissors, butterfly clips, glue, cardboard.
PREPARATION	Make a photocopy of Worksheet 3.26 for each child. Make a bus yourself as in the illustration.

Cut the cardboard up into pieces about the size of this page.

IN CLASS

1 Give each child a photocopy of the bus and a piece of cardboard.
2 Tell them to glue the photocopy on to the cardboard.
3 The children draw pictures of their family/friends in the bus windows.
4 They colour the bus as they like.
5 Make small holes in the centre of the wheels and in the places marked on the bus.
6 Help the children to fix the wheels on to their buses using the butterfly clips.

FOLLOW-UP

Sing the song 'The wheels on the bus' (see 3.9; this song is on the *Super Songs* cassette). The children could make the wheels go round as they sing the song.

VARIATION

If you cannot get butterfly clips you can use string: thread a needle with the string and make a big knot at one end. Pull the string through the wheel and then through the hole on the front side of the bus. Then make a big knot on the other side.

COMMENTS

For more on transport, see Chapter 5, 'The world around us'.

3.27 Make a robot

AGE

All

TIME

20–30 minutes

AIMS

Language: to understand instructions, to practise vocabulary for the parts of the body
Other: to practise eye–hand co-ordination, to develop creativity

DESCRIPTION

The children stick materials on to a large picture of a robot.

MATERIALS

Silver paper, sweet or chocolate papers, bottle tops, any silver food packaging, washed tops from yoghurt cartons, very large sheets of paper (one for every 8 children) with a robot sketched on (see illustration), glue.

PREPARATION

Collect the silvery materials. Draw the robot figures on the sheets of paper.

IN CLASS

1 Tell the children they are going to make a robot.
2 Spread the sheets of paper on the floor. Divide the children into groups of about eight and tell them to kneel round the pictures.
3 Give each child a stick of glue and give each group a little pile of silvery materials.
4 Tell the children they can stick the materials anywhere they like on the robot. As they work, comment in English to reinforce 'body' vocabulary: *What a nice leg! Where's his arm? Point to his arm.*
5 When they have finished, you can hang the pictures up in the classroom.

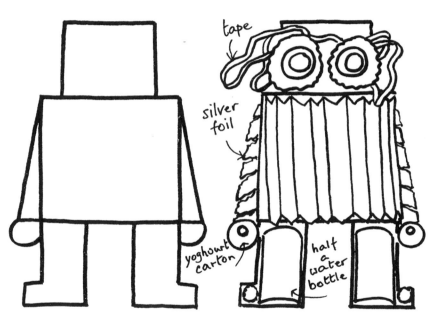

FOLLOW-UP

Sing the robot song (see 3.7) and play the robot game (see 3.18).

3.28   Cook a gingerbread man

AGE

All

TIME

20–30 minutes plus cooking time

AIMS

Language: Parts of the body, following instructions
Other: Eye–hand co-ordination, dexterity

MATERIALS

See recipe.

PREPARATION

Make a finished gingerbread man and some dough to bring to class.

Gingerbread man recipe

Ingredients   *Equipment*
200g margarine or butter   a bowl
100g icing sugar   baking tray
400g self-raising flour   aluminium foil
(or plain flour plus raising agent)   oven
1 teaspoon ground ginger
1/2 teaspoon salt
4 drops vanilla essence (optional)
Currants

Method:

1 Put all the ingredients in a bowl and mix to form a dough.

2 Roll a piece of dough into a ball between the palms of your hands and flatten it on to the aluminium foil. (This is the head.) Press on currants or make holes for his eyes, nose, and mouth.

3 Roll five more pieces into sausage shapes to form the body, arms, and legs.

4 Flatten these on to the foil, joining the pieces together by pressing them.

5 Place the foil on the baking tray and bake in a pre-heated oven (Temperature: 180° C) for about 10–20 minutes. The gingerbread men are done when they start going brown.

IN CLASS

1 Show the children your gingerbread man. Give a little bit to each child to taste.

2 Show them how to make one.

3 Let the children make more gingerbread men with the rest of the dough. Go round helping them and praising them in English, reinforcing 'body' vocabulary. Remember to mark each child's initials on her/his gingerbread man.

COMMENTS

1 Gingerbread men are a traditional favourite with children. This is an adaptation of the usual recipe to make it simpler and a better consistency for the children to handle.

2 If any of the ingredients are unavailable in the country where you teach, make up any dough mixture that you are familiar with and let the children mould men from it. You can still call it a 'gingerbread man'.

3 If there are cooking facilities in your school, you can bake the gingerbread men whilst you are telling the story in 3.20. If this is not possible, you can stack the gingerbread men in a plastic box and cook them at home. The biscuits keep for up to five days when kept in an airtight container, which means you could make them on a Friday, take them home to bake, and use them on Monday.

3.29   Gingerbread man puppet

AGE

4, 5, 6

TIME

10–15 minutes plus cooking time

AIMS

Language: to follow instructions, vocabulary for actions
Other: eye–hand co-ordination

DESCRIPTION

The children make a puppet and manipulate it during the telling of the 'gingerbread man' story (see 3.20).

MATERIALS

A photocopy of Worksheet 3.29 per child (see page 163), colours.

PREPARATION

Photocopy the puppet in Worksheet 3.29 and stick the photocopies on to cardboard. If your children have problems handling scissors you may need to cut out the puppets before the lesson.

IN CLASS

1 The children colour the puppet brown and his nose, eyes, and mouth black (for currants).
2 They then cut round the outline.
3 Make holes in the lower part of his body for their fingers to go through.
4 The children put their fingers through the holes and play with their puppet, making them walk, run, jump, etc.
5 Give the children instructions that the gingerbread men must obey: *Gingerbread man, jump!* etc.

FOLLOW-UP

The children listen to the 'The Gingerbread man' story (see 3.20), getting their puppet to run and jump at the appropriate points.

4 Number, colour, and shape

This chapter is designed to complement the children's regular pre-school classes in their first language. It helps to develop skills needed for numeracy, literacy, aesthetic ability, and the beginning of scientific understanding (for example, colour mixing).

Songs and rhymes

4.1 Ten green bottles

AGE	**All**
TIME	**10 minutes**
AIMS	**Language:** to teach/practise numbers
DESCRIPTION	The children sing a song and pretend to be the 'bottles'.
MATERIALS	A blackboard and chalk
IN CLASS	1 Draw a wall on the board. Ask the children what you have drawn and then tell them what it is in English. Draw a bottle on the 'wall'. Do the same as before telling them what it is in English. As you are drawing the other nine bottles, encourage the children to count with you: *one, two, three …*

2 Introduce the song by asking how many bottles there are. Then use a green piece of chalk to colour them. Elicit the colour.

3 Teach the song in the following way.
Point to the ten green bottles and sing:

Ten green bottles

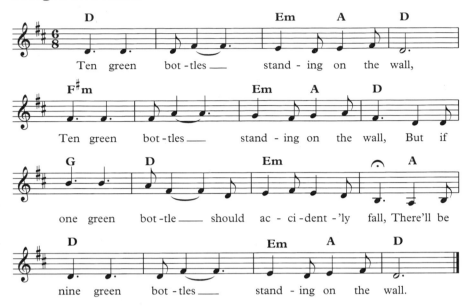

Ten green bottles standing on the wall,
Ten green bottles standing on the wall,
But if one green bottle should accidentally fall,
There'll be nine green bottles standing on the wall.
(traditional)

When the bottle 'falls', rub out the bottle on the board.

4 Sing the next verse:

Nine green bottles standing on the wall,
Nine green bottles standing on the wall,
But if one green bottle should accidentally fall,
There'll be eight green bottles standing on the wall.

When the bottle 'falls', clean it off the board.

5 Continue in the same way with the other verses until there is only one bottle left.

6 Sing the last verse as follows:

One green bottle standing on the wall,
One green bottle standing on the wall,
But if that green bottle should accidentally fall,
There'll be no green bottles standing on the wall.

7 Choose ten children to come out to the front.

8 Arrange them in a line facing the class.

9 Stand behind the child on the extreme right. Start singing the song again, encouraging the children to join in. When you come to the part: *And if one green bottle should accidentally fall …,* press down gently on the child's head and tell her/him to bob down.

10 Move along to the next child and repeat the process with the second verse.

11 Continue until all the children are down and then call out another ten children to be 'bottles'.

COMMENTS

This song is on the *Jingle Bells* cassette.

VARIATIONS

There are many traditional counting songs which you can use in class. Examples include: 'This old man', 'One man went to mow', and 'I love sixpence' (on the *Jingle Bells* cassette) and 'Ten in the bed' or 'One potato, two potatoes' (on the *Super Songs* cassette).

4.2 One, two, three, four, five

AGE

All

TIME

10 minutes

AIMS

Language: numbers, Total Physical Response, passive exposure to past simple tense

DESCRIPTION

The children sing and act out a song.

MATERIALS

A picture of a fish.

PREPARATION

Find or draw a picture of a fish.

IN CLASS

1 Show the children a picture of a fish and teach them the word.

2 Then sing the song and do the actions.

One, two, three, four, five

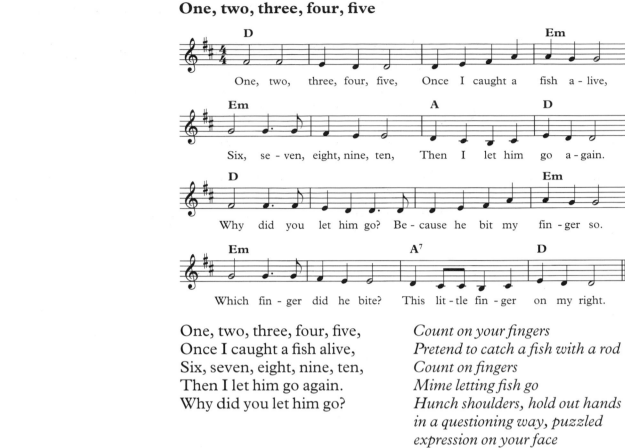

One, two, three, four, five,	*Count on your fingers*
Once I caught a fish alive,	*Pretend to catch a fish with a rod*
Six, seven, eight, nine, ten,	*Count on fingers*
Then I let him go again.	*Mime letting fish go*
Why did you let him go?	*Hunch shoulders, hold out hands in a questioning way, puzzled expression on your face*
Because he bit my finger so.	*Suck finger with a pained expression on your face, then shake your finger*
Which finger did he bite?	*Puzzled expression*
This little finger on my right.	*Shake little finger on right hand*
(traditional)	

3 Sing the song encouraging the children to join in with the actions and then with the words.

FOLLOW-UP   Play the 'Gone fishing' game (see 4.8).

COMMENTS   This song is on the *Jingle Bells* cassette.

4.3 Ten little teddy bears

AGE   **All**

TIME   **5–10 minutes**

AIMS   **Language:** to practise numbers

DESCRIPTION   The children practise the numbers one to ten, sing a song, and pretend to be teddy bears.

MATERIALS	A real teddy bear or a picture of one.
PREPARATION	See 'Teddy bear face prints' (4.12).

IN CLASS

1 Show the teddy bear and teach the word. Revise the numbers 1–10.

2 Sing the song right through, showing the numbers by holding up your fingers as you sing.

Ten little teddy bears

One little, two little, three little teddy bears,
Four little, five little, six little teddy bears,
Seven little, eight little, nine little teddy bears,
Ten little teddy bear toys.
(traditional, adapted from the song 'Ten little Indians')

3 Get the children to chant the song line by line.

4 Sing the song again, encouraging them to join in this time.

5 Bring ten children out to the front. Get them to squat down. Sing the song again, encouraging the children to join in. When everyone sings: *One little …* the first child stands up. When they sing: *Two little …* the second child stands up, and so on.

6 When they have finished, another ten children can come out.

VARIATION 1

The 'ten little teddy bears' can hide behind a door or a screen and appear as their number is called.

VARIATION 2

If you have fewer than ten children in the class then some of them could hold up cardboard 'teddy bears'.

COMMENTS

See 4.12, 'Teddy bear face prints', for how to make pictures of teddy bears. This song is on the *Super Songs* cassette.

VARIATION

You could use the song 'Five brown teddies' from the *Super Songs* cassette.

4.4   One little bird

AGE

All

TIME

5–10 minutes

AIMS

Language: numbers, passive exposure to present continuous, imperative, Total Physical Response

DESCRIPTION

The children sing a song and act it out.

MATERIALS

Four sets of wings (optional).

PREPARATION

Cut out the wings from cardboard and make slits for the children's arms to go through. Attach the two wings to each other at the back with a piece of elastic (see illustration).

IN CLASS

1   Draw a bird on the board and ask the children what it is. Then get them to say: *One little bird*. Then draw another bird and get them to say: *Two little birds*.

Draw another bird and elicit: *Three little birds*. Then draw another bird and elicit: *Four little birds*.

2   Draw a branch under the birds, point to the first bird, and say: *One little bird is sitting in a tree*. Get the children to repeat after you. Then point to two birds and say: *Two little birds are sitting in a tree*. Do the same with: *Three little birds* and *four little birds*. Make a flapping movement with your arms, clean off the first bird and say: *Fly away little bird*. Do the same with the other birds.

One little bird

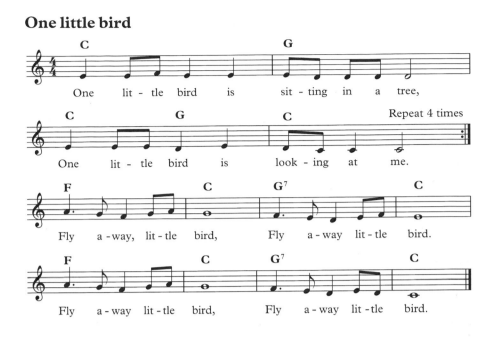

One little bird is sitting in a tree,
One little bird is looking at me.

Chorus
Fly away, little bird,
Fly away, little bird,
Fly away, little bird,
Fly away, little bird.

Two little birds are sitting in a tree,
Two little birds are looking at me.

Three little birds are sitting in a tree,
Three little birds are looking at me.

Four little birds are sitting in a tree,
Four little birds are looking at me.
(S. M. Ward)

3 Call out four children, put the wings on them, and get them to stand to one side. Point to a part of the floor and say: *This is the tree.*

4 Beckon to the first child to come and 'perch' in the tree and sing the first two lines of the song:
One little bird is sitting in a tree,
One little bird is looking at me.

(Point to your eyes to mime 'looking'.)

5 Beckon to the second child to come and perch in the tree and sing the next two lines of the song:
Two little birds are sitting in a tree,
Two little birds are looking at me.

6 Repeat step two with the third child and *three little birds.*

7 Repeat step two with the fourth child and *four little birds.*

8 Sing *Fly away, little bird* and get the first child to pretend to fly away.

9 Do the same with the second, third, and fourth children.

10 If time permits, repeat the song with four more children.

VARIATION

You could use the song 'Two little dicky-birds' from the *Super Songs* cassette.

4.5 Red and yellow, pink and green

AGE

All

TIME

10 minutes

AIMS

Language: to practise colours
Other: colour awareness

DESCRIPTION

The children sing a song about colours.

MATERIALS

Pieces of coloured card: two red, two yellow, four pink, four green, one orange, one purple, and one blue.

PREPARATION

Cut out the cards to the same size.

IN CLASS

1 If you are teaching the colours, hold up the cards one at a time and get the children to repeat the word after you. If you are revising the colours, hold up the cards one at a time and elicit the words.

2 Stick the cards on the blackboard in the order of the song.

Red and yellow, pink and green

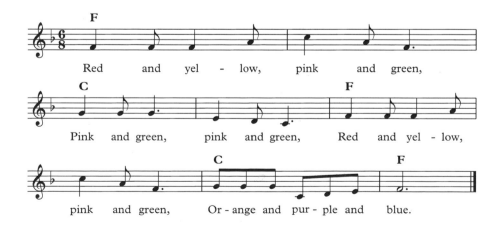

Red and yellow, pink and green,
Pink and green, pink and green,
Red and yellow, pink and green,

Orange and purple and blue.
(to the tune of 'Here we go round the mulberry bush'—traditional)

3 Chant the words with the children, pointing to the colours on the board.

4 Then sing the song through once.

5 The second time, encourage the children to join in.

4.6 Colours for you

AGE   All

TIME   **10 minutes**

AIMS   **Language:** the names of the colours
Other: colour recognition, awareness of weather

DESCRIPTION   The children sing a song about colours.

MATERIALS   Coloured chalk or a ready-made picture.

PREPARATION   You could draw the picture on the board while the children are watching, or prepare copies of Worksheet 4.6 (page 164). It should be as follows: draw some brown fields with a few trees. In the sky draw a rainbow in the same order as the the colours in the song. Round the rainbow draw some white, grey, and black clouds.

IN CLASS   1 If you have not already prepared a picture, draw one on the board according to the description above.

2 Teach the word *rainbow*. Revise the colours.

3 Sing the song doing the mimes suggested below.

4 Sing the song again, encouraging the children to accompany you with the actions.

5 Then get the children to join in with the words.

Colours for you

CHORUS

Red and or-ange and green, Yel-low, pur-ple, pink and blue,

End here

Black and white and grey and brown, These are the col-ours for you.

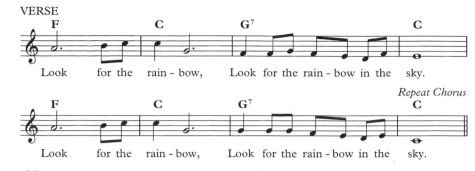

Chorus

Red and orange and green,
yellow, purple, pink and blue,
Black and white and grey and brown,
These are the colours for you.

Point to the colours in the rainbow you have drawn
Point to the clouds and fields

Sweep your hand in front of the 'rainbow' and then point to the children

Verse

Look for the rainbow,

Point to your eye then to the rainbow, and look around

Look for the rainbow in the sky,

Continue pointing to your eye and point to the sky

Look for the rainbow,

As before

Look for the rainbow in the sky.
(S. M. Ward)

As before

VARIATION 1	Make copies of Worksheet 4.6 (page 164) for the children to colour in.
VARIATION 2	An alternative song is 'Sing a rainbow' which is on the *Super Songs* cassette.
COMMENTS	For more activities on the weather, see Chapter 5, 'The world around us'.
FOLLOW-UP	Do 4.13, 'My favourite colour'.

Games

4.7   Please, Mr Crocodile

AGE	**All**
TIME	**10 minutes**
AIMS	**Language:** to listen for colours, asking permission **Other:** taking part in an organized game

DESCRIPTION

The children ask the 'crocodile' for permission to cross the 'river' and the crocodile gives permission to those wearing a certain colour. Those who are not wearing that colour try to cross and the crocodile tries to catch them.

MATERIALS

A large piece of blue material (a bed sheet) or blue paper to act as water, or two long skipping ropes to define the banks of the river.

PREPARATION

Clear an area in the classroom and place the 'water' or the 'river banks' on the floor in the middle.

IN CLASS

1 Pre-teach the question: *Please, Mr Crocodile, can we cross the river?* Explain that the crocodile only likes certain colours and he will only let you cross his river if you are wearing that colour.

2 You are the crocodile at first. Stand in the middle of the river. Say: *I'm a crocodile and I like to eat children.* Make snapping noises and look fierce. Elicit the question: *Please Mr Crocodile, can we cross the river?*

3 Choose a colour that one of the children is wearing and say: *Only if you're wearing (red).* Those that are wearing that colour can cross safely. When they have crossed, the others have to try to run across while you try to catch them. Any children caught join you as crocodiles.

4 Continue this procedure. When you feel the children are confident enough, one of them could give the instructions.

VARIATION

If your pupils wear a uniform, you could choose colour of hair or family, for example: *Only if there's a José in your family.*

4.8 Gone fishing

AGE

All

TIME

5–10 minutes

AIMS

Language: general vocabulary, *I've got a …*
Other: eye–hand co-ordination

DESCRIPTION

The children take turns to try to catch a 'fish'.

MATERIALS

Pictures from old catalogues or magazines, cardboard, paper clips, string, small magnets, some sticks, a big box or tray.

PREPARATION

Cut out small pictures from an old catalogue or magazine, for example, a watch, a bike, a doll, a radio, a television, a car, etc. Make more than enough for all the class. Stick the pictures on to small pieces of card in the shape of fish. Attach paper clips to the end of all the cards (see diagram). Make 'fishing rods': attach one

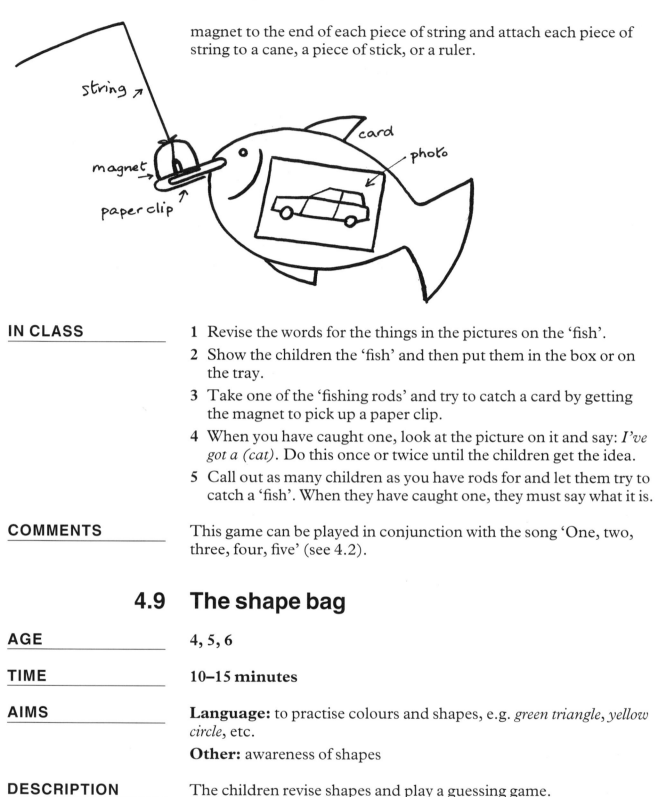

magnet to the end of each piece of string and attach each piece of string to a cane, a piece of stick, or a ruler.

IN CLASS	1 Revise the words for the things in the pictures on the 'fish'.
	2 Show the children the 'fish' and then put them in the box or on the tray.
	3 Take one of the 'fishing rods' and try to catch a card by getting the magnet to pick up a paper clip.
	4 When you have caught one, look at the picture on it and say: *I've got a (cat)*. Do this once or twice until the children get the idea.
	5 Call out as many children as you have rods for and let them try to catch a 'fish'. When they have caught one, they must say what it is.
COMMENTS	This game can be played in conjunction with the song 'One, two, three, four, five' (see 4.2).

4.9   The shape bag

AGE	4, 5, 6
TIME	**10–15 minutes**
AIMS	**Language:** to practise colours and shapes, e.g. *green triangle, yellow circle*, etc. **Other:** awareness of shapes
DESCRIPTION	The children revise shapes and play a guessing game.
MATERIALS	A bag with different coloured shapes in.
PREPARATION	Cut out triangles, circles, squares and rectangles from coloured card. Make enough so that each child has a couple of opportunities to win a shape. It is a good idea to laminate them so that you can use them over and over again.

<table>
<tr><td>IN CLASS</td><td></td></tr>
</table>

IN CLASS

1 Lay all the shapes on your desk.
2 Choose a shape and elicit the colour and shape.
3 Get the children to repeat its name in chorus, for example, *yellow square*.
4 Put the shape in the bag you prepared.
5 Do the same with all the shapes.
6 Divide the children into groups of about four or five.
7 Put the bag behind your back and take out a shape, keeping it hidden.
8 Get each group of children to guess which shape it could be. They must all say a different shape.
9 When each group has had a try, show them the shape. If one group guessed correctly give them the shape.
10 Continue until you have used up all the shapes. The winner is the group with the most shapes.

COMMENTS

As this is a game of luck it should give those children who are less competent a chance to win.

VARIATION

If you have a small class, the children need not be in groups and can guess on their own.

FOLLOW-UP

The children can make shapes out of clay or plasticine as in 'Plasticine shapes' (see 4.16).

4.10 What's the time, Mr Wolf?

AGE

4, 5, 6

TIME

10 minutes

AIMS

Language: to practise numbers and asking/telling the time
Other: to learn to play a game

DESCRIPTION

The children ask the wolf the time and she/he tries to catch them when she/he decides it is dinner time.

PREPARATION

If you have no yard, playground, or garden, you will need to clear a large area of desks and chairs.

IN CLASS

1 Teach the children the question: *What's the time, Mr Wolf?*
2 You will need to be the wolf at first. Explain to the children that you are a hungry wolf waiting for his dinner. The wolf stands with his hands on one wall and the children stand in a line with their backs against the opposite wall.
3 The children must call out: *What's the time, Mr Wolf?*

4 The wolf turns round and says the time, for example, *Two o'clock*, and then turns to face the wall again.

5 The children move forward one or two steps whilst the wolf's back is turned and ask the time again.

6 The wolf turns round and gives another time.

7 This continues until the children are fairly close to the wolf. Then, instead of giving a time, the wolf says: *It's dinner time!* She/he turns round and tries to catch one of the children before they get 'home' to the opposite wall.

8 Children can take turns at being the wolf.

COMMENTS

1 It is unlikely that children of this age will be able to tell the time, but they enjoy the game.

2 Be prepared for the children to squeal when they are being chased by the wolf—you will need to use your discretion as to how feasible this game is with a large class. When the children start running back to their 'home base', there is a risk that some of them may fall over.

Story

4.11   Red hen and brown fox

AGE

All

TIME

10–15 minutes

AIMS

Language: listening, vocabulary, *going to*, *will/won't*, passive exposure to past simple tense

DESCRIPTION

The children listen to a story.

MATERIALS

Pictures of a fox, a hen, a tree, a house, a big black bag, some stones (or a real bag and stones).

PREPARATION

Find or draw the visuals. Practise saying the story to yourself or to someone else.

IN CLASS

1 Teach the words *fox*, *hen*, *tree*, *house*, *bag*, *stones* by showing the pictures.

2 Stick the pictures up on the board where the children can see them clearly.

3 Tell the story, pointing to the pictures as they are mentioned.

Red hen and brown fox

Red Hen lived in a house in a big green tree. Brown Fox wanted to eat Red Hen so he took a big black bag and went to Red Hen's house. When Red Hen came down to get some water from the river, Brown Fox jumped up into the big, green tree and hid in Red Hen's house.

Point to the pictures as you tell the story.
Point to the pictures.
Mime getting water from a river with a bucket.
Point to picture of tree; mime climbing and hiding.

When Red Hen came back she saw Brown Fox's tail hanging out from her door, so she jumped up on to the roof.

Point to the fox's tail.
Mime jumping; point to the roof of the house.

'You can't come up here, Brown Fox,' she said. 'Go away.'

Make a dismissing gesture.

'I can't come up there,' said Brown Fox, 'but you will come down here.'

Make a beckoning gesture.

'Oh, no, I won't.' said Red Hen.

Shake your head.

'Oh, yes, you will.' said Brown Fox.

Repeat the last two lines several times—children enjoy this.

Brown Fox ran round and round and round and round and round and round … until Red Hen was so dizzy that she fell down into Brown Fox's big black bag.

Repeat this as many times as you like.
Roll your head round several times.
Mime falling down, point to bag.

'Ha, ha, ha, ha, ha, ha, ha,' laughed Brown Fox. 'I'm going to eat Red Hen for my dinner'. He jumped down from the tree and he ran and ran and ran and ran and ran and ran … until he was so hot that he had to sit down and have a sleep.

Mime jumping down.
Repeat this as many times as you like.
Wipe your brow.
Mime sitting down and sleeping.

While Brown Fox was asleep, Red Hen got out of the big, black bag and filled it with big, grey stones. Then she ran and ran and ran and ran and ran … all the way home.

Mime the actions.
Repeat as many times as you like.

Brown Fox woke up, yawned, and stretched.	*Mime yawning and stretching.*
He picked up his big, black bag and he ran and	*Mime the actions.*
ran and ran and ran … and as he ran he sang a	*Repeat as many times as you like.*
little song:	

'I'm going to eat Red Hen,
I'm going to eat Red Hen,   *Make up any tune.*
I'm going to eat Red Hen,
For my dinner.'

When Brown Fox got home he wanted to cook   *Mime the actions.*
Red Hen in a big pot of hot water, so he opened
the big, black bag and dropped the big, grey
stones into the water.

'Ow, ow, ow, ow, ow, ow, ow,' screamed Brown   *Look distressed.*
Fox as the hot water splashed all over him.

Where is Red Hen?   *Point to picture of hen.*
      Look around you.

And where do you think she was?
Yes. She was safe at home watching television.   *Mime relaxing.*

4 Tell the story again. This time point to each picture before saying the word and see if the children can call it out. Say the word again and encourage them to all say it in chorus.

FOLLOW-UP   The children can draw a picture about the story using their imagination.

Art and craft activities

4.12   Teddy bear face prints

AGE   All

TIME   10–15 minutes

AIMS   Language: following instructions
    Other: eye–hand co-ordination

MATERIALS   Paper, plates with washable ink or liquid paint (preferably brown), sponges or pads, black buttons for eyes, glue, teddy bear (optional), soap and water, overalls.

PREPARATION   1 Make a teddy bear face print yourself in advance.
    2 Sing the song 'Ten little teddy bears' (see 4.3).

IN CLASS   Show the children your teddy bear if you have one. Tell them they are going to make pictures of teddy bears' faces.

2 Give each child a piece of white paper. Give each pair of children a sponge or pad filled with paint or ink.

3 Demonstrate how to make a teddy bear face, then help the children to make one.

4 First they dip the palm of their hand in the paint or ink and press it down on the paper to make the face (keeping their fingers off the paper).

5 Then they make the ears by dipping their thumb in the paint to make three sides of a square (see the illustration).

6 Then they stick on two buttons for eyes and draw a nose.

COMMENTS

You may find it easier to do this with small groups of children at a time.

4.13 My favourite colour

AGE

All

TIME

15–20 minutes

AIMS

Language: the names of colours, following instructions

Other: awareness of colours, eye–hand co-ordination

MATERIALS

Card (different colours if possible) or white drawing paper, old magazines, scissors, glue.

IN CLASS

1 Ask each child what their favourite colour is.

2 Give them a piece of card the same as their favourite colour. Alternatively you could give them white drawing paper.

3 Show them the magazines and say they have to find things of their favourite colour.

4 They cut or tear the pictures out.

5 When they have enough to cover their card, they can stick the pictures down.

6 Make a display of their work.

COMMENTS

It is useful to have a colour display in the class which you can point to when a child gets colours mixed up.

4.14 Pockets

AGE

4, 5, 6

TIME

15 minutes

AIMS

Language: colours, following instructions

Other: to group pictures according to colour

DESCRIPTION

The children choose pictures from magazines and put them in pockets of the appropriate colours.

MATERIALS

Envelopes (approximately A5 size), coloured paper or labels, one large piece of white card (approximately A3 size) for each group, magazines, scissors, glue, a stapler.

PREPARATION

1 Collect magazines.

2 It might be a good idea to find out in a previous lesson what the children's favourite colours are to avoid disputes.

3 Prepare the posters with pockets: stick or staple four envelopes to the big piece of card. Label the pockets with the colours. Older children could help prepare the pockets.

IN CLASS

1 If you have a large class, divide them into groups. Each group needs a poster with pockets and some magazines.

2 The children cut or tear out pictures from magazines which correspond with the colours of their 'pockets'. They have to find five pictures for each colour and put them inside.

COMMENTS

Many magazine pictures of course include several colours, so be prepared to mediate in arguments or discuss interpretations of which picture is which colour.

FOLLOW-UP

The children can continue to collect pictures, adding them to their 'pockets'.

4.15 Colour mixing: magic glasses

AGE	5, 6
TIME	**10–15 minutes**
AIMS	**Language:** revising colours and objects **Other:** learning secondary colours and colour mixing
DESCRIPTION	The children learn that familiar objects seem a different colour viewed through coloured cellophane glasses.
MATERIALS	Cardboard, coloured cellophane, glue, a banana, a tomato (see Preparation).

PREPARATION

1 Make some glasses out of cardboard, using the template in Worksheet 4.15 on page 165. Make some lenses from yellow, red, green, and blue cellophane. If you cannot find cellophane you could collect sweet wrappers. You will need to divide the class into four colour groups and make the corresponding number of glasses for each group.

2 Get some objects which the children are familiar with and which have a definite colour associated with them, e.g. a banana, a tomato, etc.

3 Check with the children's other teachers to see whether they know the symbols + and =.

IN CLASS

1 Start by eliciting the name of the object, for example, *banana*. Then elicit its colour.

2 Ask the group with blue glasses to put on their glasses, look at the banana, and ask what colour they can see.

3 **(Optional)** If the children know the symbols + and =, on the blackboard draw a yellow banana and put a + sign. Then using a coloured chalk, colour a blue square. Put an = sign and then draw a green square (see diagram).

blue   green

4 Do the same with the other colour groups.

5 Repeat the procedure using different objects.

VARIATION

Take the children outside and let them look around themselves wearing coloured glasses. Help them to talk about the colours they can see.

COMMENTS

1 The concept of colour mixing is important in a child's development. Many teachers now feel it is a good idea to introduce it at pre-school level.

2 At this age we are not aiming for the children to remember the colour variations. We are merely showing them that by mixing some colours with others they can create colours. This will help in free painting classes as they will be able to experiment with secondary colours as well as primary ones.

FOLLOW-UP

Let the children mix some coloured paints in egg boxes or plastic cups and allow them some free painting time.

4.16   Plasticine shapes

AGE

All

TIME

10 minutes

AIMS

Language: the names of shapes, following instructions

Other: to encourage the children to use their hands to model

DESCRIPTION

The children make shapes out of modelling clay according to the teacher's instructions.

MATERIALS

Plasticine or other modelling materials such as clay or dough.

PREPARATION

Get enough plasticine or dough so that all the children can use it at the same time.

IN CLASS

1 Give each child a piece of plasticine.

2 Tell them to make a circle (demonstrate first if necessary). Go round observing and helping them.

3 When they have finished, do the same for other shapes like square, rectangle, triangle, etc.

VARIATIONS

You could make a simple biscuit mix (see 'Cook a gingerbread man', 3.28). The children mould the biscuit mix into shapes. You can either cook them in school if you have the facilities, or at home. Alternatively, you can make salt dough using this recipe. The children can help to make it.

COMMENTS

If you do not wish to use the dough immediately, you can keep it for a few days if you wrap it up in plastic or cling film or put it in an airtight container and store it in a cool place.

The size of the cup is not important as long as the same cup is used for each measurement.

You can cook the finished models in an oven heated to 180°C (how long for depends on the size of the model!). The children can then paint the models.

Salt dough recipe

3 cups flour

1 cup salt

1 teaspoon glycerine (not essential but it makes the dough a lot easier to work with) or 1 tablespoon cooking oil

Powder paint or food colouring (optional)

1 cup of water

A sieve

A bowl

1   Sieve the flour and salt into a bowl and add the glycerine.

2   Pour in the water, stirring continuously.

3   Continue stirring until the mixture is fairly stiff.

4   Knead the mixture together. If it is too dry, add more water and if it is too wet, add more flour.

5 The world around us

This chapter is about things that children come into contact with when they are out and about. It includes activities that will encourage children's awareness of nature, and also includes potentially frightening situations such as emergencies and going to the doctor, which can be dealt with in class through role-play. Learning about traffic signals will be an opportunity for the children to learn about other aspects of road safety.

Songs and rhymes

5.1 In and out the shops and houses

AGE   **All**

TIME   **10–15 minutes**

AIMS   **Language:** vocabulary: *shop, house, car, bus, street, take … off, clap hands, sit down, greeting friends*, Total Physical Response, passive exposure to prepositions
                   Other: co-ordination of song, rhythm, and movement, co-operative play

DESCRIPTION   The children sing a song and move round according to a set pattern.

MATERIALS   Pictures of a house, a shop, a car, a bus, a street (see the flashcards on pages 183–4).

IN CLASS   1 Teach or revise the vocabulary using the pictures.

In and out the shops and houses

In and out the shops and hou - ses, In and out the shops and hou - ses,

In and out the shops and hou - ses, On our way to school.

In and out the shops and houses,
In and out the shops and houses,
In and out the shops and houses,
On our way to school.

In between the cars and buses,
In between the cars and buses,
In between the cars and buses,
On our way to school.

Up and down the busy streets,
Up and down the busy streets,
Up and down the busy streets,
On our way to school.

Here at school we take our coats off.	*Mime*
Here at school we clap our hands.	*Clap*
Here at school we say 'Hello'.	*Shake hands*
Then we all sit down.	*Everyone sits down*

(words: L. R. Frost, to the tune of 'In and out the dusty bluebells'—traditional)

2 Choose one child to be the 'leader'.

3 Get the other children to stand in a circle, hold hands, and then raise their arms to form arches.

4 Take the 'leader' to the centre of the circle, take her/him by the hand, and sing the first verse, leading her/him in and out between the other children, under the arches.

5 When you reach the word *school*, she/he stands on the outside of the circle behind one of the others and puts her/his hands on the other child's shoulders.

6 This child weaves in and out to the singing of the second verse, followed by the first child. At the end of the verse she/he puts her/his hands on a third child's shoulders.

7 The third child leads the growing line of children in and out of the circle while all the children sing the third verse.

8 Repeat the first three verses, while more and more children weave in and out.

9 Everyone stands in a circle to sing the last verse and do the actions.

5.2 Beep beep beep

AGE	**All**
TIME	**10 minutes**
AIMS	**Language:** colours, the verb *means*, Total Physical Response **Other:** pretend play, road safety, awareness of red and green as symbolic colours
DESCRIPTION	The children pretend to drive a car and sing a song about road signs.
MATERIALS	Three pieces of card: one red, one orange, and one green.
PREPARATION	Cut out red, orange, and green circles from the card. These represent traffic lights. (If they are different colours in the country you teach in, change them accordingly.)

IN CLASS

1 Teach or revise the three colours.

2 Hold them up with the red circle on top, then the orange, then the green. Ask if anyone knows what they are. Explain that they are traffic signals we must obey if we are driving a car.

3 Teach the song, miming driving a car and holding up the appropriate colour at the right moment.

Beep beep beep

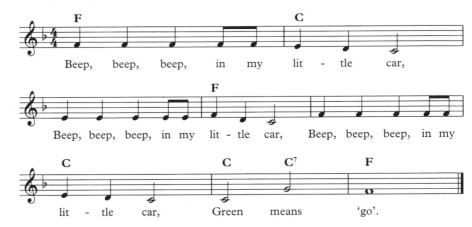

Beep, beep, beep, in my little car,
Beep, beep, beep, in my little car,
Beep, beep, beep, in my little car,
Green means 'go'.

Beep, beep, beep, in my little car,
Beep, beep, beep, in my little car,
Beep, beep, beep, in my little car,
Orange means 'slow'.

Beep, beep, beep, in my little car,
Beep, beep, beep, in my little car,
Beep, beep, beep, in my little car,
Red means 'STOP!'
(S. M. Ward)

4 Sing the song again, encouraging the children to join in the miming and singing.

COMMENTS

1 You might like to use this opportunity to talk about road safety in general and talk about where and how to cross the road according to the situation in the country where you teach.

2 Another song about transport is 'The wheels on the bus' (see 3.9).

FOLLOW-UP 1

Play the game 'Traffic lights' (see 5.12).

FOLLOW-UP 2

Teach other aspects of road safety such as crossing the road.

5.3 Sirens

AGE	**All**
TIME	**5–10 minutes**
AIMS	**Language:** names of vehicles used for emergency services, Total Physical Response
	Other: awareness of emergency services and how to phone for them
DESCRIPTION	The children talk about the emergency services and sing a song.
MATERIALS	Pictures of a fire engine, an ambulance, and a police car from the country you teach in. You could also have some pictures of British or American ones if they are available, just to show the children what they look like (see the flashcards on page 184).
IN CLASS	1 Show the children the pictures of the emergency service vehicles and ask if anyone knows what they are and when we might need to call them out. Teach them the English names.
	2 Ask children if they know which number you ring to call these services. Get them to repeat the number after you in English.
	3 Play the game 'Sirens' (see 5.13).
	4 Sing the following song, encouraging the children to join in.

Sirens

Ee-aa-ee goes the engine,
Ee-aa-ee-aa-ee.
Ee-aa-ee goes the engine,
Ee-aa-ee-aa-ee.

Chorus
Ee-aa-ee-aa-ee-aa-ee-aa,
Ee-aa-ee-aa-ee,
Ee-aa-ee-aa-ee-aa-ee-aa,
Ee-aa-ee-aa-ee.

Ee-aa-ee goes the ambulance,
Ee-aa-ee-aa-ee.
Ee-aa-ee goes the ambulance,
Ee-aa-ee-aa-ee.

(Chorus)
Ee-aa-ee goes the police car,
Ee-aa-ee-aa-ee.
Ee-aa-ee goes the police car,
Ee-aa-ee-aa-ee.

(Chorus)
(S. M. Ward)

5 Sing the song again. The children can join in and pretend to drive round while singing the song.

6 If you have a very large class you could divide them into fire engines, ambulances, and police cars, and get each group to sing their verse.

FOLLOW-UP

Sing 'London's burning' (from the *Jingle Bells* cassette), which also refers to the emergency services, and act it out.

5.4 It's raining, it's pouring

AGE

All

TIME

5–10 minutes

AIMS

Language: weather, Total Physical Response

DESCRIPTION

The children sing a song and do the actions.

IN CLASS

1 Sing or play the song and do the actions.

It's raining, it's pouring

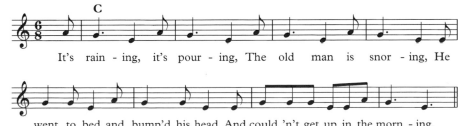

It's rain-ing, it's pour-ing, The old man is snor-ing, He
went to bed and bump'd his head And could 'n't get up in the morn-ing.

It's raining, it's pouring,	*Wiggle your fingers downwards like rain falling*		
The old man is snoring,	*Pretend to snore*		
He went to bed and bumped his head	*Lay your head on your hands and then rub your head*		
And couldn't get up in the morning.	*Pretend to try to pull your head from the pillow*		
Rain, rain, go away,	*Make a shooing movement with your hands*		
Come again another day.	*Make a beckoning gesture*		
Rain, rain, go away,	*Make a shooing movement*		
Come again another day.	*Make a beckoning movement*		
(traditional)			

2 Sing or play the song again. Encourage the children to join in.

FOLLOW-UP

Make 'Raindrop people' (see 5.18). You can also go on to do the other 'weather' activities in this chapter: 5.8, 'The weather', 5.14, 'Weather game', and 5.17, 'Weather mobile'.

COMMENTS

This song is on the *Super Songs* cassette.

5.5 Animals

AGE

All

TIME

5–10 minutes

AIMS

Language: animals, adjectives, *it likes*, action verbs, Total Physical Response

Other: awareness of animals and their characteristics

DESCRIPTION

The children learn the names of animals, mime them, and sing a song.

MATERIALS

Pictures of wild animals, including: a lion, an elephant, a crocodile, a snake, a monkey, a camel, a hippo, a parrot (see the flashcards on pages 178–82).

IN CLASS

1 Show the children the pictures and tell them the names of the animals. Do this once or twice.

2 Stick the pictures on the board in the order of the song and elicit the names from the children.

3 Ask one of the children to pretend to be a lion. While she/he is doing this, explain that we call the lion 'the King of the Jungle'. (Most children will now be aware of this because of the film *The Lion King*.)

4 Ask another child to pretend to be an elephant. While she/he is doing this describe the elephant's characteristics (big, strong).

5 Continue in this way with the other lines of the song, eliciting the description wherever possible.

6 Sing the song, miming the characteristics as suggested.

7 Sing it again a couple of times, encouraging the children to do the actions and join in.

Animals

The lion is the king of the jungle,   *Walk round looking proud*
The elephant is big and strong,   *Walk round swinging your*
                                          arm in front of your nose
The crocodile is very dangerous,   *Open and close your hands*
                                          like a crocodile's jaws
The snake is very long.   *Move your arm like a snake*
The monkey likes to swing   *Pretend to swing*
through the branches,
The camel likes to walk, walk,   *Walk round*
walk,

The hippo likes to sit in the mud all day,	*Make a gesture for 'fat' and pretend to sit*
The parrot likes to talk, talk, talk, talk, talk, talk,	*Open and close your hand like a beak*
Talk, talk, talk, talk, talk.	
(S. M. Ward)	

VARIATIONS

There are many traditional songs which mention animals, for example: 'Old MacDonald had a farm', 'The animals went in two by two', and 'Baa baa black sheep', which are on the *Jingle Bells* cassette. See also 'Ladybird, ladybird' (5.10).

5.6　Tall shops

AGE

All

TIME

5 minutes

AIMS

Language: shop, town vocabulary, prepositions, pronunciation, Total Physical Response

DESCRIPTION

The children say a rhyme and do the actions.

MATERIALS

A picture of a scene in a busy shopping street (see Worksheet 5.6 on page 166).

IN CLASS

1 Show the picture and point out the tall shops, lifts, doors, and people.
2 Say the rhyme, doing the actions.

Tall shops

Tall shops in the town,	*Hold your hand up in the air and stand on tiptoes*
Lifts going up and down,	*Reach up with your hand and then bring it down low*
Doors going in and out,	*Use your hands to motion a door swinging open and shut*
People walking all about.	*Walk around*
(© Stainer and Bell Ltd, adapted.)	

3 Say the rhyme again, getting the children to copy the actions.
4 Say the rhyme again, encouraging the children to join in.

FOLLOW-UP

Make a photocopy of Worksheet 5.6 for each child. The children colour it in. While they do so you can go round praising their work, and talking about the picture.

5.7 Incy wincy spider

AGE — All

TIME — 5 minutes

AIMS — **Language:** the weather, passive exposure to past simple tense, *up*, *down*, Total Physical Response

DESCRIPTION — The children say a rhyme and do the actions.

MATERIALS — A picture of a spider.

IN CLASS

1 Point to the spider and ask the children if they know what it is. Tell them the English word for it. Ask them if they have ever seen a spider in the bath tub.

2 Say the rhyme, doing the actions.

Incy wincy spider

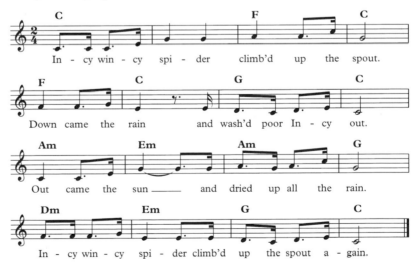

Incy wincy spider climbed up the spout.
Down came the rain and washed poor Incy out.
Out came the sun and dried up all the rain.

Spread your hand to look like a spider and make it climb up
Imitate the rain falling with your fingers
Spread your fingers over your head to represent the sun

Incy wincy spider climbed up the spout again. (traditional)	*As for the first line*

FOLLOW-UP   Make a spider as in 5.19.

5.8   The weather

AGE   **All**

TIME   **5 minutes**

AIMS   **Language:** vocabulary about the weather
Other: Total Physical Response

DESCRIPTION   The children say a rhyme about the weather and do the actions.

MATERIALS   Four pictures to represent the snow, the rain, the sun, and the wind (see Worksheet 5.17 on page 168).

PREPARATION   Prepare the pictures.

IN CLASS
1 Show the picture of the snow and say: *It's snowing.* Wrap your arms around yourself and shiver (as in the song below). Get the children to repeat.
2 Repeat this procedure with the other pictures.
3 Put the pictures up on the board in the order of the rhyme.
4 Say the rhyme, doing the actions.
5 Repeat a couple of times, encouraging the children to join in.

Weather rhyme

It's snowing, it's snowing,	*Move your hands downwards slowly wiggling your fingers*
Brr, brr, brr,	*Wrap your arms round yourself and shiver exaggeratedly*
It's raining, it's raining,	*Move your hands downwards quickly, wiggling your fingers*
pit-a-pat, pat,	*Tap your fingers lightly on the top of your head*
It's sunny, it's sunny,	*Spread your fingers out and sweep them in a big circle over your head*
Phew! Phew!	*Pretend to wipe the sweat from your brow*
It's windy, it's windy,	
Whoosh! Whoosh!	*Fill your cheeks with air and make a whistling or blowing sound*
(V. Reilly and S. M. Ward)	

FOLLOW-UP 1   The children can make 'Weather mobiles' (see 5.17) and play the 'Weather game' (see 5.14).

FOLLOW-UP 2   When the children come to school each day, ask them *What's the weather today?* The children can record each day's weather using a big calendar and the symbols from the weather mobile in 5.17, or make a 'Weather clock' as in *Young Learners* by S. Phillips, in this series, page 120 (see Further Reading).

5.9   Miss Polly had a dolly

AGE   **All**

TIME   **5 minutes**

AIMS   **Language:** *doctor*, *sick*, *pill*, passive exposure to past simple tense, Total Physical Response
Other: talking about illness

DESCRIPTION   The children say or sing and act out a rhyme.

MATERIALS   A doll.

IN CLASS   1 Show the children the doll. Put your hand on her forehead and pretend that it is very hot. Say: *My dolly is very sick. What shall I do?* Let the children make suggestions.

2 Tell the children that you are going to say a rhyme about a sick dolly. Say or sing the rhyme, doing the actions suggested.

Miss Polly had a dolly

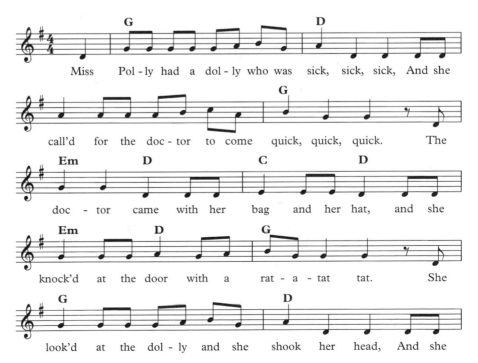

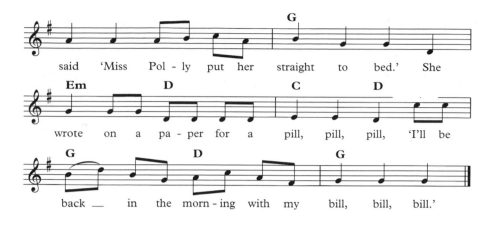

Miss Polly had a dolly who was sick, sick, sick,	*Rock the doll in your arms*
So she called for the doctor to be quick, quick, quick,	*Pretend to phone*
The doctor came with her bag and her hat,	*Pretend to swing a bag and take a hat off*
And she knocked on the door with a rat-tat-tat.	*Rap your knuckles on the table*
She looked at the dolly and she shook her head	*Look solemn and shake your head*
And she said 'Miss Polly, put her straight to bed.'	*Wag your finger and mime putting the doll to bed*
She wrote on a paper for a pill, pill, pill,	*Mime writing on the palm of your hand*
'I'll be back in the morning with my bill, bill, bill.'	*Make whatever gesture is customary for paying in the country you teach in*

(traditional)

3 Say the rhyme again, encouraging the children to do the actions with you.

4 Call out two children to be the doctor and Miss Polly. They do the actions while you recite the rhyme. Encourage the other children to join in with words like *sick, sick, sick*.

5 Let other children do the mime. Do not insist on the children reciting the whole rhyme—the important thing is that they understand what it says. If you repeat it in subsequent classes, they will pick up on other words.

VARIATION

You can use this rhyme instead:

Mother, mother I feel sick

Mother, mother I feel sick.
Send for the doctor quick, quick, quick.
In came the doctor, in came the nurse.
In came the lady with the alligator purse.

FOLLOW-UP 1

The children play 'Going to the doctor's' (5.11).

FOLLOW-UP 2   The children colour in the picture strip of the story in Worksheet 5.9 (page 167).

COMMENTS
1 The doctor can be male or female.
2 You can chant the rhyme or sing it along to the music. The music is included on the *Super Songs* cassette.

5.10   Ladybird, ladybird

AGE   **All**

TIME   **5 minutes**

AIMS   **Language:** pronunciation
Other: awareness of wildlife

DESCRIPTION   The children say a rhyme about a ladybird.

MATERIALS   The ladybird from 5.20 or a picture of one.

PREPARATION   Make the ladybirds from 5.20 (optional).

IN CLASS
1 Show a picture of a ladybird. If they do not exist in the country where you teach, compare them with the nearest equivalent.

2 Tell the children they are going to say a rhyme about a ladybird.

Ladybird, ladybird

•   •   •   •
Ladybird, ladybird, fly away home,

  •   •   •   •
Your house is on fire, your children are gone.

•   •   •   •
All except one; her name is Ann

  •   •   • •
And she has crept under the frying pan.
(traditional)

3 Get the children to repeat the rhyme after you line by line. Tell them what it means.

4 If you have made the ladybirds from 5.20, the children can pretend to make their ladybirds fly and act out the story.

Games

5.11 Going to the doctor's

AGE	**All**
TIME	**15 minutes**
AIMS	**Language:** to learn to say what is wrong when they are not well **Other:** to role-play
DESCRIPTION	The children learn how to describe common ailments and role-play being at the doctor's.
MATERIALS	An overall, a toy stethoscope (if available) or an improvised one with a bit of rubber or plastic tubing; a picture of a doctor.
IN CLASS	**1** Show the picture of the doctor and ask the children if they know who it is and if they have ever been to the doctor's. Ask if they know the name of their doctor. (This stage could take quite a long time if the children want to regale you with all the illnesses

they've had. You will need to use your own discretion depending on how long the lesson lasts.)

2 Hold your head and start moaning: *Oh, oh, I've got a headache.* Then hold your stomach, moan, and say: *I've got stomach-ache.* Then put your hand on your jaw and say: *I've got toothache.* Wipe your brow and say: *I've got a temperature.* Pretend to sneeze and say: *I've got a cold.*

3 Do this once or twice then call out one of the children. Say: *I've got a headache* and see if she/he can mime the action. Do this with other children and the other expressions.

4 Call out one of the children to do a mime and the other children have to say: *headache, toothache* etc.

5 Drill the sentences, getting the children to mime as they say them.

6 Put on the overall and put the stethoscope round your neck and say: *I'm the doctor.* Ask for a volunteer to come out and be the patient.

7 Ask the 'patient': *What's the matter with you?*

8 Get her/him to mime and say: *I've got …*

9 Pretend to write a prescription and say: *Here you are.*

10 Repeat this with one or two more children and then let them do the role-play in pairs.

5.12 Traffic lights

AGE	**All**
TIME	**10–15 minutes**
AIMS	**Language:** colours, following instructions, Total Physical Response
DESCRIPTION	The children pretend to be cars and go fast or slow or stop according to which traffic sign is shown.
MATERIALS	One green, one red, and one orange circle of cardboard (or whatever colours are used in the country where you teach).
PREPARATION	Prepare the circles.
IN CLASS	1 Hold up the green circle and elicit the colour.
	2 Do the same with the orange and red circles.
	3 Get the children to form a circle round you and tell them that they are driving cars. They must walk round you quickly when you say 'green', slowly when you say 'orange' and they must stop when you say 'red'.
FOLLOW-UP	This game ties in with the song 'Beep beep beep' (see 5.2).

5.13 Sirens game

AGE	**All**
TIME	**10–15 minutes**
AIMS	**Language:** vocabulary: *fire engine*, *police car*, *ambulance*; listening, Total Physical Response **Other:** to learn to call the emergency services
DESCRIPTION	The children learn about the emergency services and play at being ambulances, fire engines, and police cars.
MATERIALS	Pictures of the vehicles of the emergency services (see the flashcards at the end of the book), a toy telephone (if available).
PREPARATION	Get the pictures of the vehicles.

IN CLASS

1 Show the children the pictures and teach or revise the names in English.
2 Ask the children what noise these vehicles make.
3 Discuss when we might need to call them.
4 Give each child a role: *You're a fire engine. You're a police car. You're an ambulance.*
5 Get the children to stand at one end of the room or yard. You stand at the other end with the toy telephone. Pretend to ring the emergency number, saying it aloud in English. (Use your local one.)
6 Then you say: *Can you send an ambulance, please?* All the 'ambulances' run (or walk if you think running is too dangerous) to your end of the room.
7 Send them back and repeat the procedure with 'fire engines' and 'police cars'.
8 When the children are familiar with the procedure, they might like to take turns to use the phone.

FOLLOW-UP

This game ties in with the song 'Sirens' (see 5.3).

COMMENTS

Most small children are fascinated by the noise made by the vehicles of the emergency services. Some are frightened by them, especially if they associate them with some dramatic event in their own lives. Playing at being ambulances, fire engines, etc. might help the children to see them as less threatening.

5.14 Weather game

AGE	**All**
TIME	**10–15 minutes**
AIMS	**Language:** to understand instructions, to revise words for clothes and the weather, Total Physical Response **Other:** to encourage independence in putting on clothes, doing up buttons, zips, etc.
DESCRIPTION	The children revise vocabulary for weather and clothes and play a game in which they have to choose the appropriate clothes for the weather.
MATERIALS	Clothes suitable for all seasons from the dressing-up box. Pictures of snow, wind, sun, and rain (see Worksheet 5.17, page 168).
PREPARATION	In previous lessons teach the words for different types of clothing from the class situation (e.g. *Susan's wearing a pink dress today.*) Teach the weather on a day-by-day basis (see 5.8) and through pictures, books, or videos.

IN CLASS

1 Revise weather vocabulary using pictures, and clothes using the ones that the children are going to put on in the game.

2 Put all the clothes in the centre of the room and get the children to fetch you the right item when you say, for example, *Louis, go and find a hat.*

3 After practising this a few times, tell the children that you are going to play a game in which they have to choose the right clothes according to the weather. Then you say, for example: *Kumiko, it's raining.* Kumiko must go and find something suitable for a rainy day. If she brings something suitable, she can wear it but if it is unsuitable, she must take it back. If you think the children would like a competition, the person who is wearing the most clothes at the end of the game is the winner.

VARIATION	Older children might like to play this game in teams once they are familiar with it.
COMMENTS	This game could take a lot longer with the youngest children.
FOLLOW-UP	Make a 'Weather Mobile' (5.17) and 'Raindrop People' (5.18).

5.15 Animal movements

AGE	**All**
TIME	**10–15 minutes**
AIMS	**Language:** to listen for instructions, words for animals and the way they move, Total Physical Response **Other:** learning about animals
DESCRIPTION	The children learn the words for animals and the way they move. They then play a game in which they imitate the animals.
MATERIALS	Pictures of the following animals: a kangaroo, a bird, a camel, a snail, a snake, a jaguar, a horse (see the flashcards on pages 177–82). A recording of some instrumental music (e.g. *The Carnival of the Animals* by Saint-Saens). If you like you can make animal masks as in 6.15.
PREPARATION	If you think it is preferable, teach the words for the animals in previous lessons.
IN CLASS	1 Show the pictures of the animals and teach or elicit the names for them. 2 Show the picture of the kangaroo and say: *Kangaroos jump.* (Jump up and down to illustrate the meaning.) 3 Show the picture of the kangaroo again and say: *Kangaroos jump.* Indicate that you want the children to do the action. 4 Repeat stages 2 and 3 with the following: *Birds fly. Camels walk. Snails crawl. Snakes wriggle. Jaguars run. Horses gallop.* (If you think there are too many, you could save some for another occasion.) 5 Put the instrumental music on and the children start walking round the room. When you call out the name of an animal, they must do the appropriate movement. 6 If you wish, divide the children into groups of different animals. When you call out the name, only those in that group do the action.
VARIATION	On another occasion you could use the sounds that animals make instead of the way they move. For example: *Dogs say woof woof. Cats say miaow. Pigs say oink oink. Birds say tweet tweet. Snakes say Sssssssss. Horses say neigh.* If you prefer, you can use the animal sounds that the children are familiar with in their own language, although they do like learning the English equivalents.
FOLLOW-UP	Sing the 'Animals' song (see 5.5).

Stories

5.16 The hare and the tortoise

AGE — **All**

TIME — **10–15 minutes**

AIMS — **Language:** narrative, animal vocabulary, comparatives, listening
Other: following a story

DESCRIPTION — The children listen to a story.

MATERIALS — A picture of a hare and a tortoise and other animals (see the flashcards on page 167).

PREPARATION — Before you start the story, draw a hill on the board with a path going up to the top.

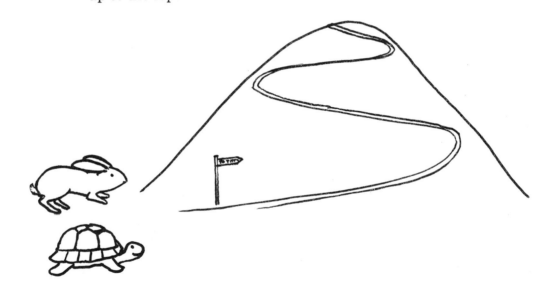

IN CLASS —
1 Hold up pictures of a hare and a tortoise and say what they are (in English). Ask if the children have ever seen one. Elicit/explain that hares can run very fast, but tortoises can only walk very slowly (mime these actions).
2 Tell the story, miming the actions.

3 Repeat the story, encouraging the children to join in the actions.
4 Pairs of children can mime the story as you tell it again.
5 The children draw pictures of the hare and tortoise.

VARIATION — You can move a cardboard cut-out hare and tortoise on a felt or Velcro board to illustrate the story as you tell it.

One day the tortoise was walking slowly along the road.

Hold up the picture of the tortoise and pretend to be the tortoise walking slowly along.

Suddenly she saw the hare, who was running and skipping along.

Show the picture of the hare and mime running and skipping.

When the hare saw the tortoise she began to laugh: 'Ha, ha, ha. You are so slow.' The tortoise said; 'Yes, I'm slow but nothing stops me. Look. Do you see that hill?'
'Yes', said the hare. 'I can see it. So what?'

Point to the hill on the board.

'Well, I'll race you to the top.' said the tortoise.

Run your finger up the path from the bottom to the top.
You can give the names of different animals here.

'Ha, ha, ha,' laughed the hare. 'You race me? That's great!
Ha, ha, ha.' Then the hare called all her friends.

'Hey. Come on everybody,' she said, 'We're going to have a race. Come and watch us.' All the other animals came and the hare and the tortoise lined up.

Beckon
Show the pictures of other animals and elicit or say their names.

The fox said: 'Ready, Steady, Go!' and the hare went running off.

Mime this.

Meanwhile the tortoise started walking slowly along: plod, plod, plod, plod, plod, …

Mime this.

After a while the hare stopped and turned around. She looked down the hill. There was the tortoise a long, long, long, long, long way away.

Mime this.
Shield your eyes and look down; and into the distance.
Point.

'Ha, ha, ha,' said the hare. 'That tortoise will never catch me up. I've got time to have a little sleep.' So she sat down under a tree, closed her eyes, and went to sleep.

Laugh.

Mime these actions.

Meanwhile the tortoise carried on walking: plod, plod, plod, plod, plod, plod, plod, plod, plod … Suddenly she heard someone snoring.

Mime the tortoise plodding.
Cup your hand to your ear.
Make the noise of someone snoring.

'Who's that?' She looked round and there was the hare fast asleep under a tree.

Look around; point.
Mime being asleep.

'Ha, ha, ha,' said the tortoise. 'She thinks she's better than me.' And she carried on walking up the hill: plod, plod, plod, plod, plod, plod …

Laugh and walk slowly on.

After some time the hare woke up. 'Where's the tortoise?'she said. She stood up and looked down the hill.

Mime waking up, standing up, looking down the hill.

She could not see the tortoise anywhere. Then she turned round and there was the tortoise at the top of the hill!

Mime turning around, look surprised.

'Ha, ha, ha,' shouted the tortoise. 'Slow but sure wins the race.'

Raise your arms to celebrate winning.

All the animals at the bottom of the hill clapped and shouted 'Hooray! Good old Tortoise!'

Clap and encourage the children to join in.

Art and craft activities

5.17 Weather mobile

AGE   4, 5, 6

TIME   **20 minutes**

AIMS   **Language:** to revise weather vocabulary, to follow instructions
                   Other: manual dexterity and eye–hand co-ordination

DESCRIPTION   The children colour and make a weather mobile.

MATERIALS   One copy of Worksheet 5.17 per child (see page 168), a coat-hanger
                   (or a piece of stick or a straw) per child, sewing cotton, sticky tape,
                   coloured pencils or crayons.

PREPARATION   Make photocopies of Worksheet 5.17. If your pupils are very young
                   you may want to perforate round the pictures with a sewing
                   machine to make it easy for them to tear out.

IN CLASS   1 Hand out photocopies, revise the weather words, and tell the
                      children to colour the pictures.
                   2 When they have finished colouring, they cut or tear round the pictures.
                   3 They stick some sewing cotton to each picture with sticky tape as
                      in Figure 1.
                   4 They tie the sewing cotton to the hangers or sticks or straws at
                      different intervals along them as in Figure 2.

Figure 1   *Figure 2*

VARIATION	Use the pictures to make a weather chart (see 5.8).
COMMENTS	This activity follows on from 5.4, 'It's raining, it's pouring' or 5.14, 'Weather game'.

5.18   Raindrop people

AGE	**All**
TIME	**10 minutes**
AIMS	**Language:** to follow instructions, to revise vocabulary **Other:** eye–hand co-ordination
DESCRIPTION	The children colour and cut out 'raindrop people'.
MATERIALS	A large picture of a raindrop for each child.
PREPARATION	Draw two huge raindrops like the illustration. Make enough copies for each child to have one raindrop.

IN CLASS	1 Give each child a picture of a raindrop. 2 Tell the children to colour the raindrop any way they like and to draw a face on it. 3 When they have finished colouring, they can cut or tear round the outline. 4 They can stick the 'raindrop people' on a sheet of paper, or attach sewing cotton as in 5.17 and make mobiles. If you attach them to different lengths of cotton and hang them from the ceiling, it will look like rain falling.
COMMENTS	This activity can follow on from the song in 5.4, 'It's raining, it's pouring'.

5.19 Spiders

AGE	5, 6
TIME	**10–15 minutes**
AIMS	**Language:** to follow instructions, to revise vocabulary
	Other: eye–hand co-ordination, learning to use scissors
DESCRIPTION	The children learn to make a spider from a paper cup.
MATERIALS	A paper cup for each child, scissors, black powder paint mixed with a little glue, elastic.
PREPARATION	Make a spider to show the children the finished product.
IN CLASS	1 Give each child a paper cup.
	2 Get them to colour it black.
	3 While you are waiting for the cups to dry you could do the rhyme 'Incy wincy spider' (see 5.7).
	4 Show the children how to cut the cup as in the illustration.

5 The children paint the eyes on the spider.

6 Make a hole in the bottom of each child's cup and show them how to thread the elastic through and tie a knot at one end, so that they can make their spiders go up and down.

VARIATION 1	Children of 3 or 4 could make a spider using hand prints. They put their hands in black paint and press their palms on to a sheet of paper with their four fingers outstretched. They then turn the paper round and do the same again (see illustration).
VARIATION	Another way of painting spiders is to put a daub of black paint in the middle of a sheet of paper and fold it over. This will make a big shapeless blob. The children then add four legs each side of the blob.

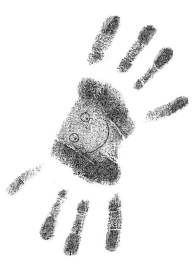

5.20   A ladybird

AGE

4, 5, 6

TIME

10–15 minutes

AIMS

Language: to follow instructions
Other: eye–hand co-ordination

DESCRIPTION

The children make a ladybird.

MATERIALS

Photocopies of the ladybird from Worksheet 5.20 on page 169 (one for each child), black and red crayons, scissors, glue.

IN CLASS

1 Give each child a photocopy of the ladybird.
2 Tell them to colour the ladybird's body red and to colour its head and spots black.
3 The children cut round the ladybird and its wings. You will have to be careful to make sure they do not cut tabs A and B off. You may need to do that bit for them.
4 Show the children how to stick tabs A and B in the correct places. Again you may need to help them with this.
5 If there is time, or in another lesson, you could organize a 'ladybird race'. Two children at a time blow their ladybirds across a smooth surface (such as a table) and see which is the winner.

6 Festivals

Festivals are a good way of introducing children to the culture of the countries where English is spoken. Children also enjoy the celebrations immensely and can get very excited. We have included Christmas, Carnival, and Easter in this chapter as they are very popular with young children and they lend themselves to games, dressing up, and colourful activities to which family and friends can be invited.

Although these three festivals are part of the Christian calendar, many of the elements are based on ancient pagan celebrations and many of the ideas could be adapted to other festivals, such as a dragon procession for Chinese New Year or making presents for Eid ul-Fitr. For children of pre-school age the main interest lies in Christmas presents, Easter eggs, and Carnival processions, and the celebrations need not have any religious significance at all. Whether or not you include these or other festivals is at your discretion depending on your teaching situation.

Christmas

Christmas is a festival which is very important for children in many countries where English is spoken. In schools many hours are dedicated to decorating the classroom, preparing school concerts and nativity plays, and making Christmas cards to send to family and friends. It is perhaps the most important festival for children: full of colour, fun, and surprises. Children mark the days off on a calendar until Christmas Eve (24th December), when Father Christmas brings presents in the night. Usually children get up very early on Christmas Day (25th December), often having only slept a couple of hours, to see what Father Christmas has brought them. They then spend the day with their family eating turkey, Christmas Pudding (a hot cake-type dessert with raisins and other dried fruit), and lots of chocolate.

6.1   Twinkle twinkle little star

AGE	**All**
TIME	**10 minutes**
AIMS	**Language:** to sing a traditional song **Other:** to link music and hand movements
DESCRIPTION	A traditional nursery rhyme.
MATERIALS	A star (see 6.8), string, sticky tape.
PREPARATION	Make a star with the class. Cut some string of different lengths. Stick a piece of string to each star using sticky tape. Tie the stars at intervals to a length of string. Put the string up across the classroom like a washing line—make sure it is high enough so that you can walk about without the stars touching your head.

IN CLASS

1 Sing the song, doing the actions.

Twinkle twinkle little star

Twinkle, twinkle, little star,	*Start with fists closed then open your hand on each word*
How I wonder what you are.	*Point and look upwards and look puzzled*
Up above the world so high,	*Point to the stars*
Like a diamond in the sky;	*Put fingers in a 'diamond' shape*
Twinkle, twinkle, little star,	*Start with fists closed then open your hand on each word*
How I wonder what you are.	*Look at the stars and stroke your chin pensively*

(traditional)

COMMENTS

1 The star is an important element in the Christmas story (see 6.9, 'Nativity play'). Stars are used as decorations and often put at the top of the Christmas tree (see 6.7).

2 This song is on the *Super Songs* cassette.

6.2   O Christmas tree

AGE   **All**

TIME   **10 minutes**

AIMS   **Language:** vocabulary: Christmas, weather
                      Other: physical co-ordination

DESCRIPTION   A traditional Christmas song.

IN CLASS   1 You could play 5.14, 'Weather game', to introduce the idea of the
                         seasons. If not you will have to present the vocabulary from the
                         song by showing pictures to the children.
                      2 Sing or play the song and do the actions. Then sing it again,
                         encouraging the children to join in.

O Christmas tree

O Christmas tree, O Christmas tree,	*Make your arms into a triangle shape by joining your hands*
How lovely are your branches.	*Repeat the previous action*
O Christmas tree, O Christmas tree,	*Repeat the previous action*
How lovely are your branches.	

In summer sun or winter snow,

Hold out your hands above your head with fingers open like the sun's rays, and then bring them down, moving your fingers like snow

A coat of green you always show.

Pretend to close your coat around you

O Christmas tree, O Christmas tree, How lovely are your branches. (traditional)

Repeat the actions

FOLLOW-UP   You could continue the theme of the Christmas tree with the rhyme 'Here is the tree' (6.4), and then make a Christmas tree as in 6.7.

COMMENTS   A Christmas tree is a small fir tree decorated with coloured baubles, tinsel, and lights.

6.3   I'm a fairy doll

AGE   **All**

TIME   **15 minutes**

AIMS   **Language:** toy vocabulary
Other: singing

DESCRIPTION   The children sing a song.

MATERIALS   Pictures of different toys (see flashcards)

IN CLASS   1 Teach the children the rhyme 'I like toys' (see 3.15).

2 Use the pictures to teach the children some more names for different toys.

3 Sing the song.

I'm a fairy doll

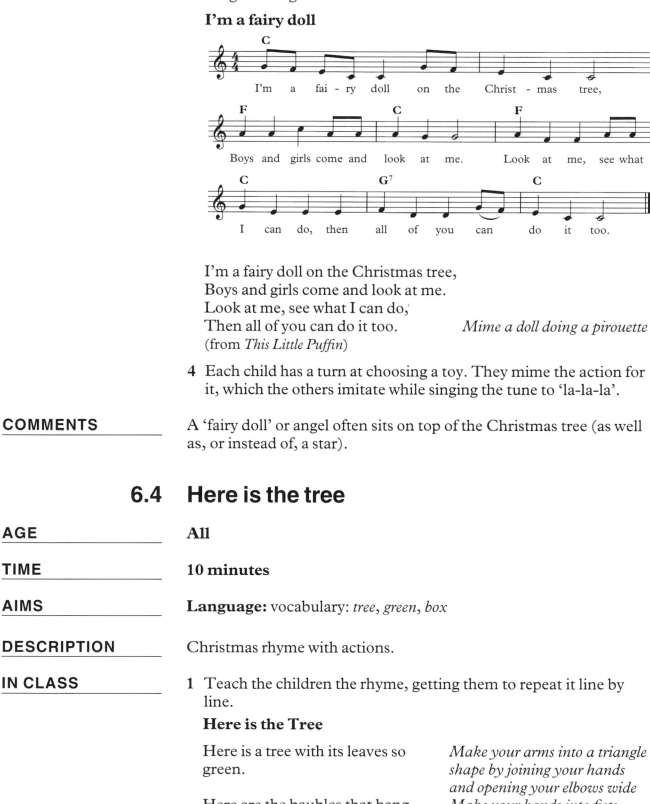

I'm a fairy doll on the Christmas tree,
Boys and girls come and look at me.
Look at me, see what I can do,
Then all of you can do it too.   *Mime a doll doing a pirouette*
(from *This Little Puffin*)

4 Each child has a turn at choosing a toy. They mime the action for it, which the others imitate while singing the tune to 'la-la-la'.

COMMENTS

A 'fairy doll' or angel often sits on top of the Christmas tree (as well as, or instead of, a star).

6.4 Here is the tree

AGE

All

TIME

10 minutes

AIMS

Language: vocabulary: *tree*, *green*, *box*

DESCRIPTION

Christmas rhyme with actions.

IN CLASS

1 Teach the children the rhyme, getting them to repeat it line by line.

Here is the Tree

Here is a tree with its leaves so green.

Make your arms into a triangle shape by joining your hands and opening your elbows wide

Here are the baubles that hang between.

Make your hands into fists

When Christmas is over, the baubles will fall. Here is a box to gather them all. (traditional, adapted)	*Let your fists drop down* *Join your arms in front of you making a circle*

6.5   Pull the cracker

AGE — **All**

TIME — **10 minutes**

AIMS — **Language:** rhythm
Other: to introduce the children to a British tradition

DESCRIPTION — The children chant a rhyme.

MATERIALS — A picture of the cracker to show the children.

PREPARATION — Make a cracker before the lesson (see 6.10) or bring one in if you have one.

IN CLASS —

1 Show the cracker to the children and explain that it is something British people have at Christmas. When we eat our Christmas meal, two people each pull one end. Crackers make a bang when they break.

2 Say the rhyme and get the children to do the actions.

Pull the cracker

Pull the cracker. BANG!	*Pretend to pull and then say 'BANG!' loudly*
Pull the cracker. BANG!	*Repeat the actions*

Do not run and hide.	*Shake your head*
Let's see what's inside.	*Pretend to look inside something*
Pull, pull, pull the cracker.	*Actions as before*
BANG!	
(E. Yorke and M. Robinson)	

FOLLOW-UP   Older children can make a cracker as in 6.10.

COMMENTS   A cracker is a Christmas decoration which contains a small gift, a party hat, and a joke or message. Two people hold either end of the cracker and pull. One of them wins the gift by pulling harder than the other.

6.6 Guess the present

AGE   **All**

TIME   **15 minutes**

AIMS   **Language:** *What is it?*, shapes, colours, vocabulary

Other: to guess something by its shape

DESCRIPTION   A guessing game.

PREPARATION   Make the 'presents'. Draw or find pictures of objects that are reasonably easy to guess by their outline. Cut them out and stick them to cardboard. On the other side stick some pretty paper.

IN CLASS
1 Tell the children that you have some presents and they must guess what they are.
2 Hold up a 'present' with the pretty paper facing the children and ask them to try and guess what it is.
3 The child who guesses correctly holds the picture.
4 The child with most 'presents' is the winner.

COMMENTS   Some children will shout out the answers. Give quieter children a chance to win a 'present' too.

6.7 Make a Christmas tree

AGE   **All**

TIME   **20 minutes**

AIMS   **Language:** to revise colours

Other: eye–hand co-ordination

DESCRIPTION	The children make a pretend tree.
MATERIALS	Triangles of green card, sweet papers, bottle tops, and other pieces of bright junk.
IN CLASS	1 Show the children one of the green triangles and ask them what they think they are going to make.
	2 Fold the triangle in half and stand it up. If they cannot guess then tell them they are going to make a Christmas tree.
	3 Ask them which colours they expect to see on a Christmas tree.
	4 Show them the bright papers, etc. you have collected and get them to tell you the colours they want on the tree. Stick decorations to your tree as they tell you.

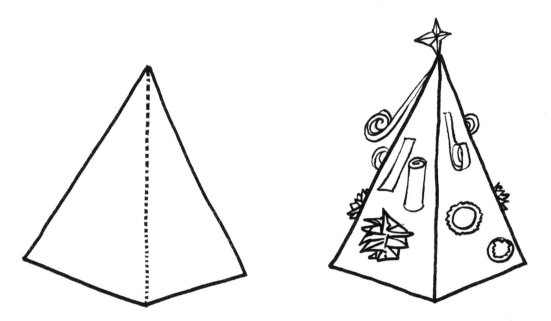

5 The children now make a tree themselves.

VARIATION 1	If your children are just learning the colours and are not very confident at speaking, you could convert it into a listening exercise by telling them which colours to take from the pile of papers.
VARIATION 2	Put one big green triangle on the wall, low enough for the children to reach. All the children help to decorate the class 'tree'.

6.8 Christmas star

AGE	4, 5, 6
TIME	**20 minutes**
AIMS	**Language:** *star*, following instructions **Other:** eye–hand co-ordination

DESCRIPTION	The children make a star to decorate the classroom or Christmas tree.

MATERIALS	Photocopies of stars (see Worksheet 6.8 on page 170), aluminium foil, scissors.

PREPARATION

1 Make a star before the lesson to show the children.
2 Photocopy Worksheet 6.8 on to pieces of card if possible (otherwise stick paper stars on to card). Cut out enough star shapes for all the class.
3 Also cut some pieces of aluminium foil that are about the size of the star.

IN CLASS

1 Show the children the star you have made and say: *This is a star. Today we are going to make a star.*
2 Give each child a star.
3 Show them how to wrap the foil round the star.
4 The children then do this.
5 Write each child's name on their star.
6 Hang the stars up (see instructions in 6.1).

FOLLOW-UP	Sing 6.1, 'Twinkle twinkle little star'.

6.9 Nativity play

AGE	**All**

TIME	**Several lessons to practise, 20 minutes for the performance**

AIMS

Language: listening to instructions, for example, when organizing the play:

Who wants to be …?, Here's a …, Where are your (wings) Susanna?

when rehearsing the following phrases might be useful:

Move backwards/forwards., Stand near., Kneel down, Give the … to ….

to learn English phrases by heart and say them out loud.

Other: confidence, performing in public

DESCRIPTION

The children act in a play of the Christmas story—the birth of Christ (called a Nativity play). This is very common in British schools. Children enjoy taking part; they love dressing up and it gives them a chance to perform on stage. Relatives willingly help to prepare costumes and then proudly go and watch the children perform.

MATERIALS

Mary normally wears a blue dress and a white headscarf.
Joseph and the shepherds wear robes (dressing gowns or pieces of material with holes for their heads) and a headscarf kept in place with a tie or cord.

The angels wear white dresses and wings cut out of white card (see 4.4). (The wings can also be made with a bed sheet. Tie a knot in the middle of the sheet. Fix the knot to the child's back with a safety pin. The child then holds the top two corners of the sheet).

The kings wear fancy robes (silk dressing gowns, or a bright piece of material with a hole cut in the middle for the child's head). Crowns can be made from card. One king can wear a turban made from bright material.

The kings carry presents made from boxes, one covered in gold paper to represent gold and the other two wrapped in brightly coloured paper.

The shepherds give toy sheep and other toy animals.

A baby doll to represent the baby Jesus.

Chairs. A box with straw for a 'crib' for the baby.

A star, stuck or pinned on the wall or on a curtain high up over the 'crib'.

PREPARATION

1 Tell the children that the whole class is going to put on a Christmas play. Ask for volunteers and choose which children will play the main speaking parts. It is not difficult to give all children a part as there can be a number of angels and shepherds. If there are too many children to fit on the stage, some could form a choir and sing Christmas songs. So they do not feel left out of the dressing-up they could dress like the angels. Not all the children will want a speaking part and they should not be pressurised into taking part if they are unwilling. Some can be 'stage managers' and help to move the 'props'.

2 Tell the children the story. Teach them their 'lines'. All the children can learn the main characters' lines, although only a few will speak in the play.

3 Collect everything you need. Ask the children to bring costumes and dolls. Keep a record of who brought what so that you can return it afterwards.

IN CLASS

Rehearse the play several times—you will need several lessons. Invite parents for the performance.

FOLLOW-UP

The children can colour in the nativity scene in Worksheet 6.9 (page 171).

Nativity play

This is just a suggestion as to how the play might be performed. You can adapt it to your own situation.

Characters
Mary
Joseph
The innkeeper
Angel Gabriel   Other angels
Chief shepherd   Other shepherds
Kings: Gaspar, Melchior, Balthasar

Place two chairs and the crib on the right of the stage. Hide the baby doll under Mary's chair.
Mary and Joseph walk on to the stage from the left and Joseph pretends to knock on a door. The innkeeper appears.

Joseph: Have you got a room?
Innkeeper: No, I haven't, but here's a stable. (*Points to the two chairs and the crib.*)
Joseph: Thank you very much. *Mary and Joseph go and sit down. Mary takes the baby doll, rocks it gently, and then puts it in the crib.*
Mary: My name's Mary and this is baby Jesus.
Joseph: My name is Joseph and this is my family.

The shepherds come on to the stage from the left and sit down. The angels appear and the shepherds look afraid.

Chief shepherd: (*to Gabriel*) Oh! Who are you?
Gabriel: I'm the Angel Gabriel. Come with me to see the baby Jesus.

The shepherds follow Gabriel across the stage. Gabriel goes behind Mary and Joseph and stands on a chair as though in the air. The shepherds kneel down one by one to present their gifts.

Shepherds: Here's a gift for the baby Jesus.

The three kings enter on the left and cross the stage .
They kneel down one by one to present their gifts.

Gaspar: I'm Gaspar. Here is gold for the baby Jesus.
Melchior: I'm Melchior. Here is frankincense for the baby Jesus.
Balthasar: I'm Balthasar. Here's myrrh for the baby Jesus.

6.10   Crackers

AGE	4, 5, 6
TIME	20 minutes
AIMS	**Language:** *s*to listen to instructions
	Other: to develop hand co-ordination
DESCRIPTION	The children make something typical to celebrate Christmas by listening to instructions from their teacher.
MATERIALS	Pieces of thin card cut into pieces of 15cm by 10cm, pieces of crepe paper 30cm by 20cm, strips of string or ribbon, sweets, and sweet papers to decorate.

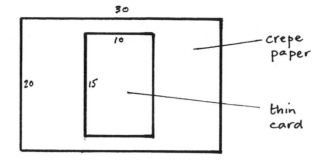

IN CLASS

1   Bring the children round a desk where they can all see what you are doing and tell them what to do whilst showing them.

2   First place the crepe paper on the table.

3   Then place the piece of card in the middle of the paper (see diagram).

4   Now put some sweets in the middle and start to roll the cracker into a tube.

5   Ask one of the children to hold the cracker and tie a piece of string or ribbon as close as possible to the card.

6   You will have to help the children to tie the ribbon. However, it is well worth all the hard work.

7   Finish decorating the cracker by gluing sweet papers on to it.

The children can take their crackers home if they celebrate Christmas.

FOLLOW-UP

Chant 'Pull the cracker' (see 6.5).

Carnival

In many countries Carnival is celebrated in the early spring and usually consists of processions of lorries decorated with imaginative scenes. Some of the most famous Carnival processions are held in Rio de Janeiro and Cadiz on Shrove Tuesday. People wear fancy dress and dance through the streets to music. In Britain, this day is normally only celebrated by the cooking and eating of pancakes. In Britain, Carnival processions take place in different towns at different times of the year, usually in the summer months. The most famous of these is Notting Hill Carnival, which is organized by the West Indian community and is held in late August.

6.11 Carnival song

AGE	**All**
TIME	**10 minutes**
AIMS	**Language:** vocabulary associated with Carnival: *mask, costume, dance, dragon, clown, giant,* etc. Use of *going to* **Other:** using imagination and creativity. Co-ordination of language–rhythm–dance.
DESCRIPTION	The children practise language connected with Carnival, sing a song, wear masks (optional), and form a dancing dragon.
MATERIALS	Pictures or a video-clip of a Carnival procession (see Worksheet 6.11, page 172), masks (optional), home-made musical instruments (optional)
PREPARATION	Find pictures or a video-clip of a Carnival procession. If you want to, make musical instruments (see Comments), hats (see 6.12), or masks (see 6.15).
IN CLASS	1 Show the children pictures or a video-clip of a Carnival procession. Elicit words and supply those they do not know. 2 Sing the song to the children, encouraging them to clap the rhythm. 3 Sing the song again. When you come to the part: *I'm going as …,* invite the children to supply a character (e.g. *Batman, Pocahontas,* etc.) and then include it in the song. If you do not want them to all shout out at once, ask individual children. The children may want to pretend to be the character. 4 Sing the song a few times, letting different children make suggestions and encouraging them to join in. If the children have brought or made masks, they can shout out the character that their mask represents. 5 The children form a dragon. Each child puts her/his hands on the shoulders of the child in front and they dance round the class singing the song. (The older ones might manage this wearing masks if the eye-holes are big enough, but it could be too dangerous for three-year-olds.)

Everybody loves carnival

Ev -'ry-bo - dy loves Car - ni -val.— We're going to have — a par - ty, We're going to have — a par - ty, We're going to have — a par - ty, And I'm going as (Bat -man)! (Pocahontas)! etc. Car -ni -val, — Car -ni -val, — Ev -'ry-bo - dy loves Car - ni -val. — Car -ni -val, — Car -ni -val, — Ev -'ry-bo - dy loves Car - ni -val. —

Chorus
Carnival, Carnival,
Everybody loves Carnival.
Carnival, Carnival,
Everybody loves Carnival.

We're going to have a party,
We're going to have a party,
We're going to have a party,
And I'm going as …
(S. M. Ward)

COMMENTS

Before the lesson you could improvise some instruments and get some of the children to be a 'band'. Plastic bowls or buckets can be used as drums, wooden spoons as castanets, plastic containers filled with rice or beans can be maracas, and some children can hum into combs with paper placed in front.

FOLLOW-UP 1

The children all dress up as their favourite characters and have a procession round the classroom or school. They can make hats as in 6.12 or masks as in 6.15.

FOLLOW-UP 2

The children colour in the picture of a Carnival procession in Worksheet 6.11 (page 172).

6.12 Pirate hat

AGE	**All**
TIME	**15–20 minutes**
AIMS	**Language:** following instructions **Other:** eye–hand co-ordination
DESCRIPTION	The children make a pirate hat.
MATERIALS	One sheet of newspaper for each child, black poster paint, one skull and two crossbones cut out of white paper for each child, sellotape, a paintbrush for each child, glue.

PREPARATION

1 Cut one skull and two bones out of white paper for each child, as in the illustration.

2 Make a hat in advance to show the children.

IN CLASS

1 Demonstrate how to make the hat, getting the children to copy each step. The hat is made as follows:

a Fold the newspaper in half.

b Turn down the two corners on the folded part.

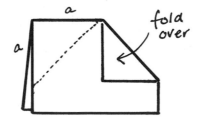

c Fold up the two bottom flaps.

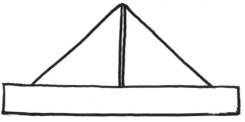

d Fold the corners of the flaps round and seal with sellotape.

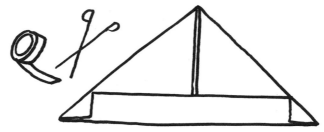

2 Tell the children to paint the outside of the hat with black paint.

3 Stick a skull and crossbones on each hat as in the illustration.

VARIATION 1

If you want to make Robin Hood hats, paint them bright green instead of black and stick a feather on the side of the hat.

VARIATION 2

If you want to make a clown hat, colour it all different colours and stick a paper pom-pom near the top.

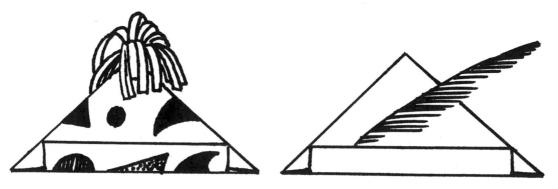

VARIATION 3

Older children could help make the skulls and crossbones, but this will add some time to the lesson.

COMMENTS

Little children love wearing hats. These hats could be used for Carnival and other festivals or for drama activities and pretend play.

Easter

Although Easter is an important Christian festival, the traditional symbols such as eggs, chicks, and rabbits are celebrations of spring. In some places the Easter Bunny (rabbit) brings chocolate eggs on Easter Sunday. In Britain, on Easter Monday (the following day) there are many different traditional games and contests such as Hunt the Egg, Egg Rolling, Egg and Spoon Races, and Egg Painting. Some villages compete against each other with 'Tug-of-War' (rope pulling) or ball games.

6.13 Hot cross buns

AGE	**All**
TIME	**5 minutes**
AIMS	**Language:** following instructions, food
	Other: singing

Hot cross buns

450g white flour	1 egg, beaten
25g fresh yeast	100g dried fruit
150ml tepid milk	milk to glaze the top of the buns
60ml tepid water	1 level teaspoon of salt

half a teaspoon each of mixed spice, cinnamon, and nutmeg

50g of caster sugar

50g butter, melted and cooled but not firm

1 Sift 100g of flour into a large bowl. Mix the yeast with the milk and water, stir it into the flour and leave in a warm place for 15–20 minutes, until frothy. Sift the remaining flour, salt, spices, and sugar into a large bowl.

2 Add the butter, egg, flour mixture, and dried fruit to the yeast mixture and mix to a soft dough.

3 Turn on to a floured surface; knead until smooth.

4 Put in a large greased bowl, cover with oiled polythene; leave to rise until it has doubled in size.

5 Turn on to a floured surface and knead.

6 Divide the dough into pieces and roll them into balls.

7 Arrange them well apart on floured baking tray, cover, and leave for 30 minutes.

8 Bake at 190°C/375°F for 15/20 minutes.

DESCRIPTION

The children sing a traditional Easter song. A Hot Cross Bun is a sweet bun made with dried fruit, which has a cross marked on the top. It was traditionally eaten on Good Friday but it is now eaten at other times.

MATERIALS

Ingredients for the buns (optional).

PREPARATION

If you would like to show the children what hot cross buns are, you can make some before the lesson.

IN CLASS

1 Tell the children that at Easter people in Britain eat hot cross buns and tell them that they are going to make some.

2 If possible let the children shape their bun.

3 Take a piece of dough and show them how to roll it into a ball using the palm of your hand. Then press down to flatten it a little and finish it off by drawing a cross on top.

4 Put the buns on the baking tray and leave, as in the recipe.

5 Sing the song whilst the buns are rising and cooking.

Hot cross buns

Hot cross buns, hot cross buns.
One a penny, two a penny,
Hot cross buns.
If you have no daughters,
Give them to your sons.
One a penny, two a penny,
Hot cross buns.
(traditional)

6 Get the children to join in.

7 When the buns have cooled down the children can try them.

FOLLOW-UP   You can talk about food special to festivals in your country.

COMMENTS   This song is on the *Jingle Bells* cassette.

6.14 Story: Why do rabbits have long ears?

AGE   **All**

TIME   **15–20 minutes**

AIMS   **Language:** listening, names of animals, *I'm a …*, *You're a …*

DESCRIPTION   The children listen to a story.

MATERIALS   Pictures of rabbits and other animals (optional—see the flashcards on pages 177–82).

PREPARATION   Before you start the children could make masks so that they can join in more with the story (see 6.15, 'Animal Masks').

IN CLASS   1 Divide the class into six groups and get each group to sit together.

2 Tell the children that in many English-speaking countries the Easter Rabbit takes chocolate eggs to the children. Ask the children what a rabbit looks like. To introduce the story, tell them that rabbits have not always had long ears and that you are going to tell them how they got long ears.

3 Tell the story. You will need to use a lot of mime to give some visual back-up to the words.

Why do rabbits have long ears?

Once upon a time the King of the Animals decided to give all the animals names.

He said, 'You're a lion'	*Point to one group.*
'You're a monkey'	*Point to the second group.*
'You're a crocodile'	*Point to the third group.*
'You're a frog'	*Point to the fourth group.*
'You're a tiger'	*Point to the fifth group.*
'You're a hippo'	*Point to the last group.*
And finally he said to the rabbit, 'You're a rabbit	*Point to yourself.*

But rabbits have terrible memories and rabbit could not remember his name. 'Oh no! I can't remember my name.' So he went to the King and said, 'I'm sorry. I can't remember my name.' 'You're a rabbit', said the King. 'Oh, thank you!' said the rabbit. The rabbit went away. 'I'm a rab-ra-r. Oh, no! I can't remember my name.'

So the rabbit went to the king and said, 'I'm sorry. I can't remember my name.' 'You're a rabbit', said the King. 'Oh, thank you!' said the rabbit and went away.

'I'm a rab-ra-r. Oh, no! I can't remember my name.' So the rabbit went to the King. 'I'm very sorry,' said the rabbit, 'but I can't remember my name.' The King was angry and he shook the rabbit by the ears, 'You're a rabbit, rabbit, rabbit.'

'Oh, yes. I'm a rabbit.'

The Rabbit went for a walk and he saw a . . . .

Point to the first group of children and try and elicit 'lion'.
Elicit 'lion'; then get the children to ask 'What's your name?'

'What's your name?' said the Rabbit.
'My name's . . . .
The Rabbit said, 'My name's rab-ra-r. Oh, no! I can't remember my name. Goodbye!' Suddenly his ears grew just a little bit. And he continued until he saw . . . .

Repeat the same procedure for all the animals, eliciting the names from all the groups.

The rabbit's ears were long and he suddenly remembered the King. 'My name's rabbit. Hello hippo, my name's rabbit. Hello ...'

Continue greeting all the groups of animals.

And that is how rabbits got long ears.

FOLLOW-UP 1   Tell the story again, letting the children pretend to be different animals: jumping like a frog or hopping like a rabbit. Children love to act out this story and to wear animal masks (see 6.15).

FOLLOW-UP 2   Children can make rabbit puppets using the same technique as in 3.29, 'Gingerbread man puppet'.

FOLLOW-UP 3   The children can invent their own stories about other animals.

Acknowledgements
This story is adapted from one in *jet* magazine called 'Mr Rabbit's long ears'.

6.15   Animal masks

AGE   4, 5, 6

TIME   **15–20 minutes**

AIMS   **Language:** names of animals, colours
                   Other: hand co-ordination, colouring in

DESCRIPTION   The children make masks to act out the story 'Why do rabbits have long ears?' (6.14).

MATERIALS	Photocopies of the masks (see Worksheets 6.15A–6.15C, pages 173–5), coloured pens/pencils, cardboard.

PREPARATION — Photocopy Worksheets 6.15A–6.15C for the groups of children. Other animal masks can be made by adapting these (see the illustration).

IN CLASS

1 Divide the class into their groups for the story (see 6.14). Give them the names of their animals: *Group 1—lions, Group 2—monkeys*, etc.
2 Talk about the animals, for example, *What colour is it? What colour eyes has it got?* etc.
3 Give the masks to the groups.
4 The children colour them.
5 Stick the masks to card and cut round them. If your children have problems with cutting and sticking, you could do this before the lesson so they just have to colour in.
6 Put elastic on the masks to hold them on.

FOLLOW-UP — Do 5.15, 'Animal movements'.

6.16 Can you find the eggs?

AGE — 4, 5, 6

TIME — **5–10 minutes**

AIMS — **Language:** *Where is/are …*, prepositions
Other: observation, colouring in

DESCRIPTION

A typical activity for children at Easter is to go on an egg hunt. An adult hides a chocolate egg and the children have to find it. As this could prove a bit hectic in a class of 30 children it may be better for the children to find the eggs in a picture.

PREPARATION

Photocopy the picture on Worksheet 6.16 (page 176) for each child—or you could make a poster by photocopying it on to A3 paper.

IN CLASS

The children must find the eggs. Encourage them to tell you where the eggs are.

FOLLOW-UP

The children colour in the picture.

6.17 Egg and spoon race

AGE

4, 5, 6

TIME

15 minutes

AIMS

Language: following instructions: *Hold the spoon*, *ready*, *steady*, *go*, *run*, *don't drop the egg*, *come on Kate*, etc.

Other: eye–hand co-ordination, taking part in a team game

DESCRIPTION

The children have a team race while holding an egg on a spoon.

MATERIALS

4 wooden spoons or dessert spoons, 4 hard-boiled eggs or ping-pong balls.

IN CLASS

1 Divide the class into four or five teams.

2 Get the members of each team to stand one behind the other and line up the first member of each team so that they are level.

3 Give the first member of each team a spoon with an egg in it.

4 Tell the children that they have to run (or walk) to the board (or wall) without dropping the egg, touch the board, return, and hand the spoon with the egg in it to the second member of their team. They must use only one hand while racing but if they drop the egg, they can put it back in the spoon and continue.

5 When the second member of the team returns from touching the

board, she/he hands over the spoon and egg to the third member of the team and so on until all the members of the team have done it.

6   The last member of each team must bring the spoon to you. The first team to do so is the winner.

COMMENTS	1 Children can get very excited and noisy while playing this game so it is better if you can play it outside. 2 Make sure no children cheat by holding the egg with their finger.

6.18   Egg painting

AGE	**All**
TIME	**15 minutes**
AIMS	**Language:** revision of colours, following instructions **Other:** eye–hand co-ordination
DESCRIPTION	The children decorate eggs.
MATERIALS	One hard-boiled egg per child and one for the teacher, coloured crayons or pencils (not paints or pens if the children are going to eat them afterwards, as eggs are porous).
IN CLASS	1 Revise colours by showing the colours and eliciting the names for them (see Chapter 4, 'Number, colour, and shape'). 2 Show the children how to decorate an egg. 3 Give each child an egg and let them decorate it in any way they want.
FOLLOW-UP	The children can have an egg rolling competition. 1 Draw a mark on the floor. 2 Each child takes a turn at rolling her/his egg towards the mark from a particular point. 3 The child who gets her/his egg closest to the mark is the winner.
VARIATION	The children can paint the eggs with food colouring, or dye them with special edible dye.
COMMENTS	1 You will probably have to ask parents to provide the eggs. 2 When the eggs have been coloured, they can be eaten as long as the colour has not penetrated the shell and marked the white of the egg. But the children may want to keep their eggs.

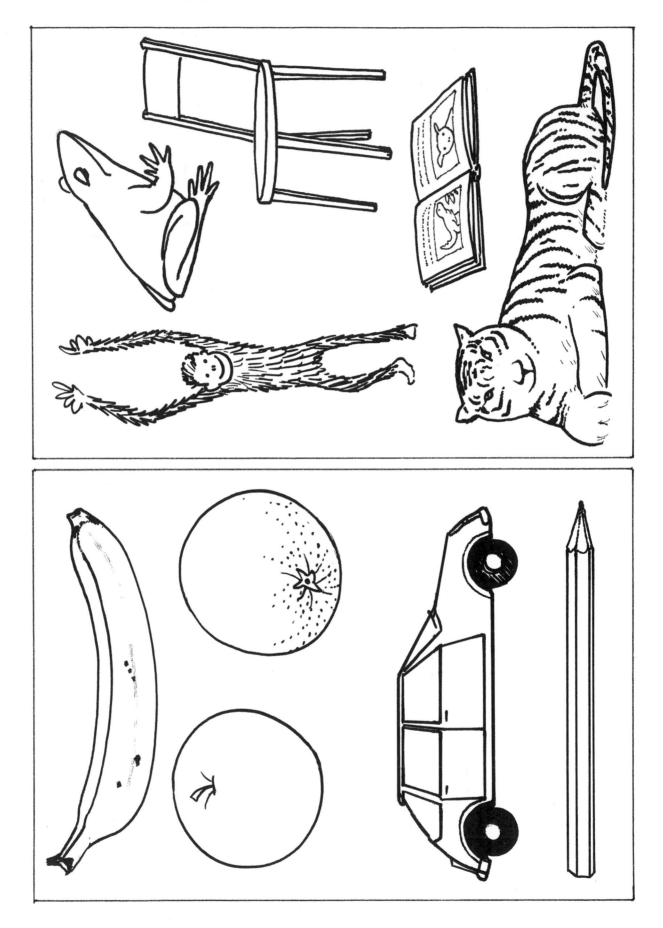

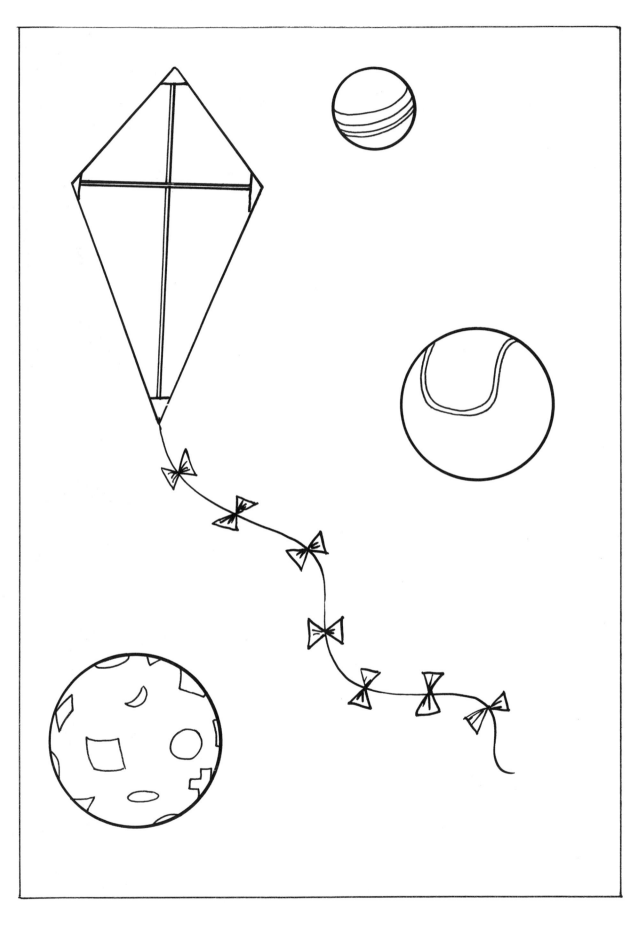

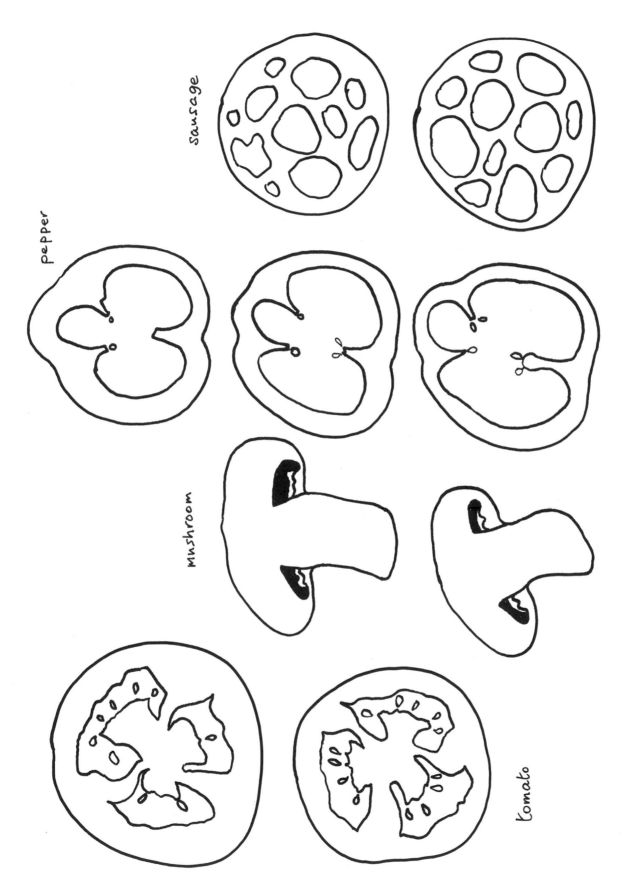

sausage

pepper

mushroom

tomato

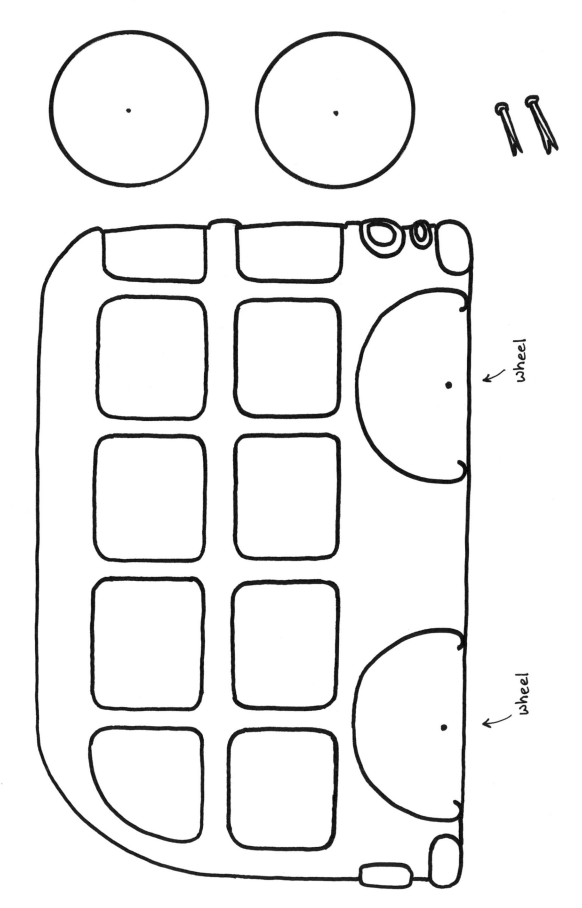

wheel

wheel

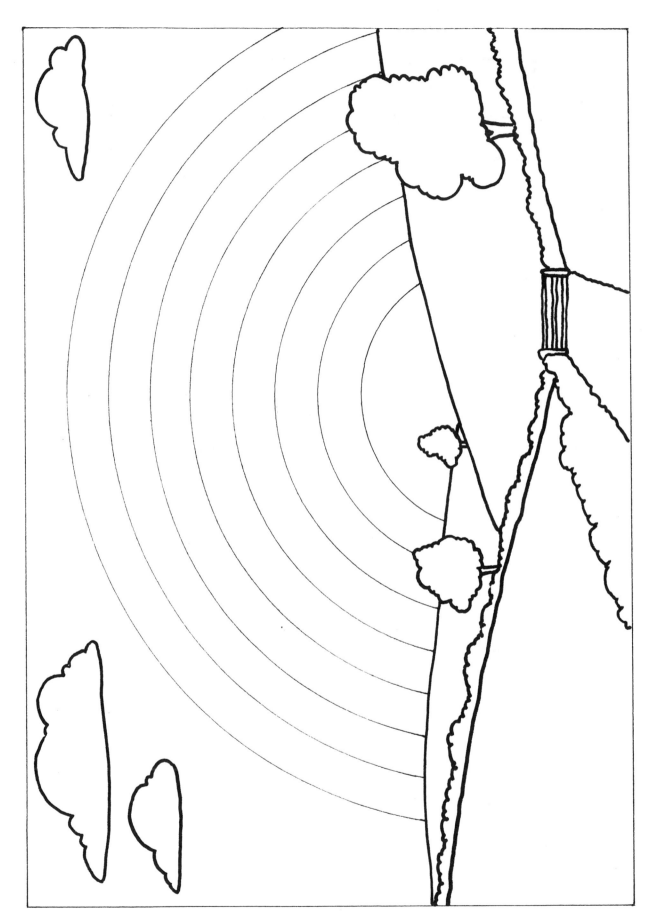

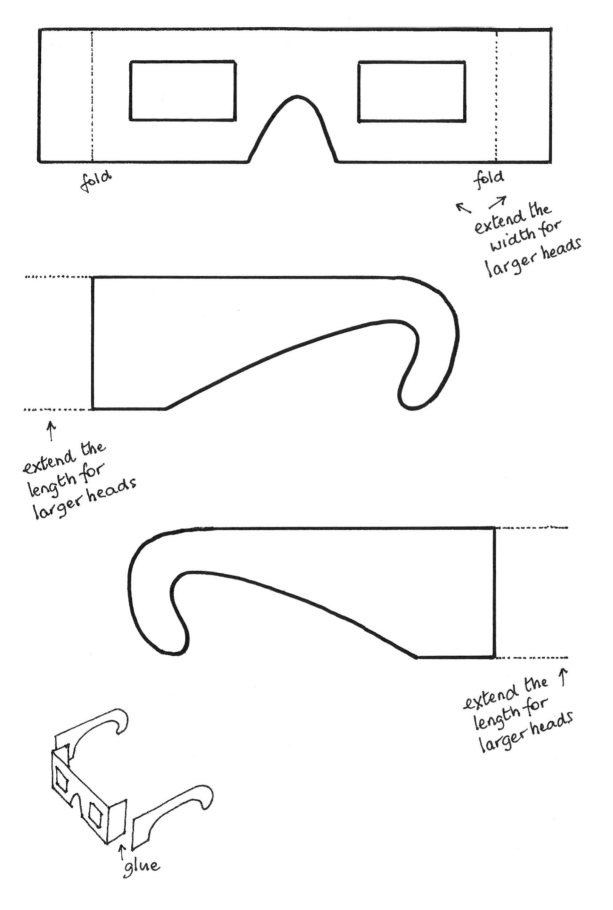

fold

fold

extend the
width for
larger heads

extend the
length for
larger heads

extend the
length for
larger heads

glue

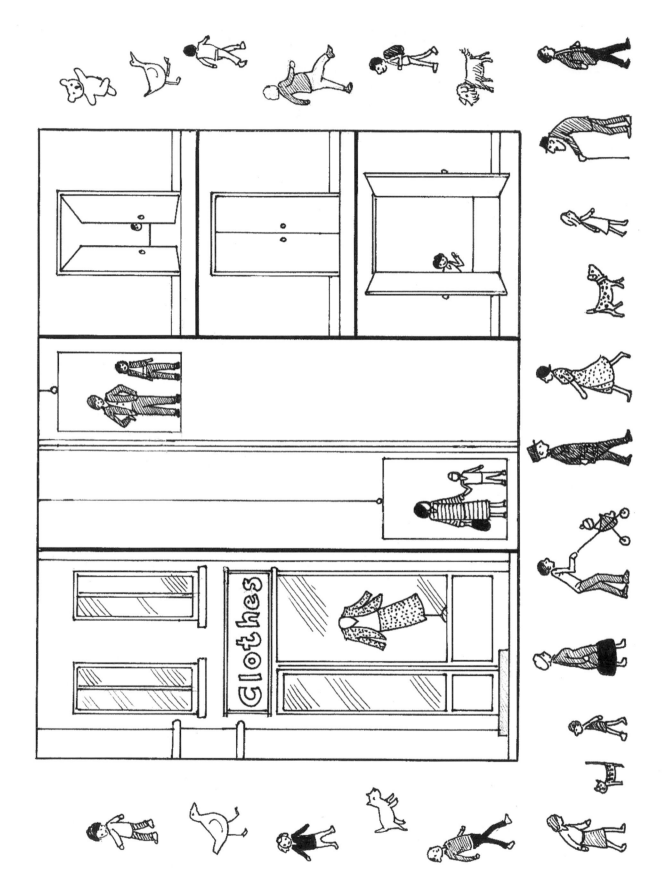

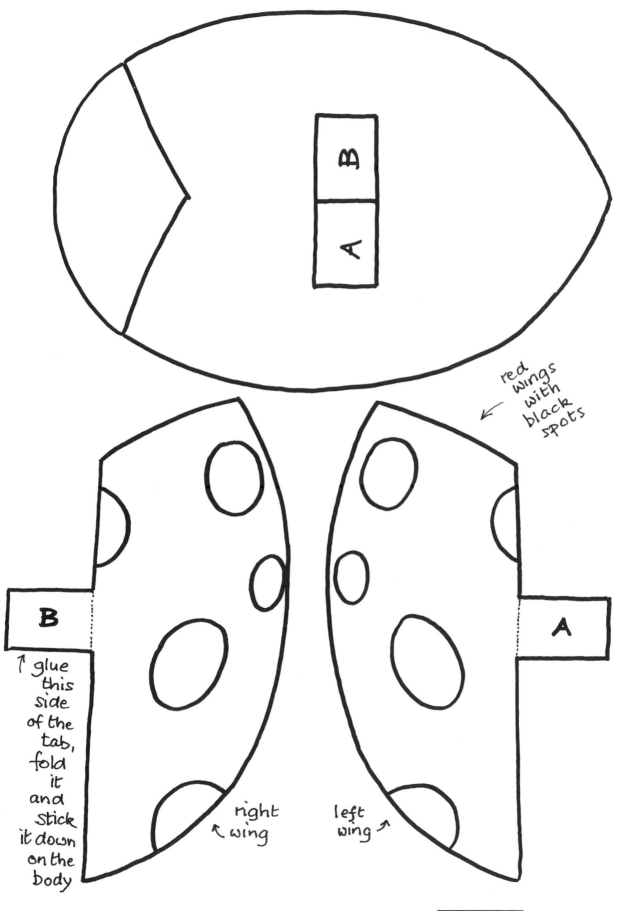

B

A

red
wings
with
black
spots

B

A

↑ glue
this
side
of the
tab,
fold
it
and
stick
it down
on the
body

right
↖ wing

left
wing ↗

Hole for
string or
elastic

Cut out
the eyes

Hole for string or elastic

Cut out the eyes and the nose

Hole for string or elastic

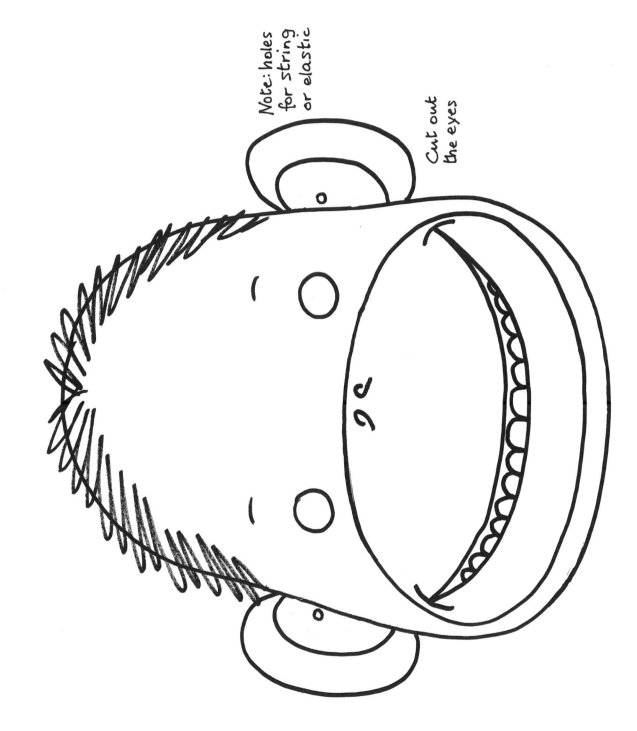

Note: holes for string or elastic

Cut out the eyes

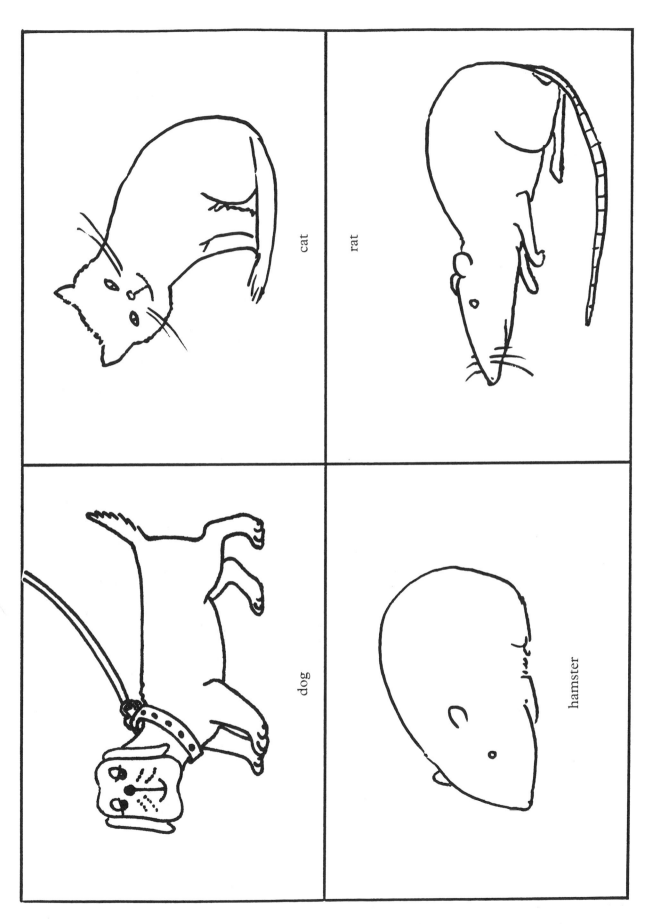

cat

rat

dog

hamster

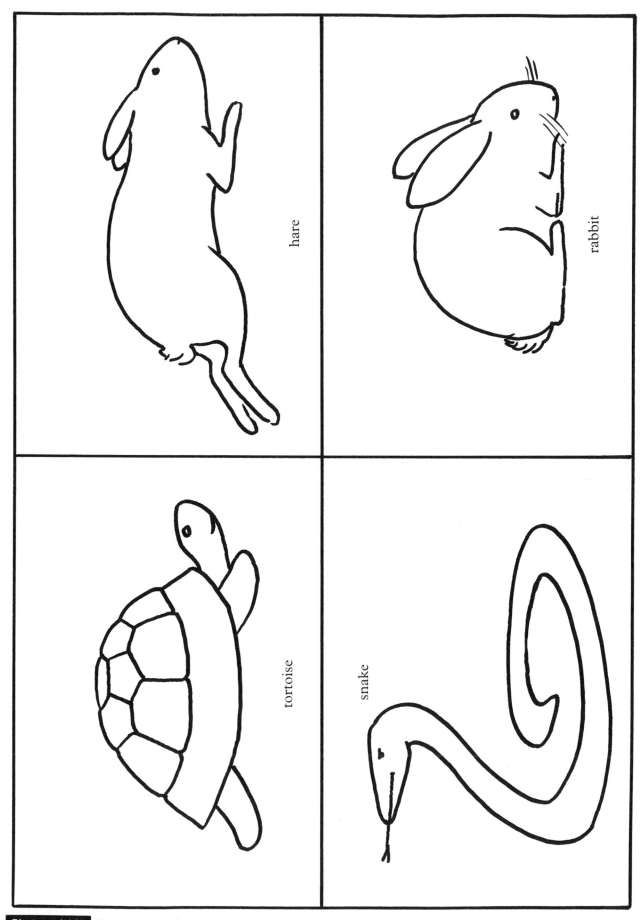

hare

rabbit

tortoise

snake

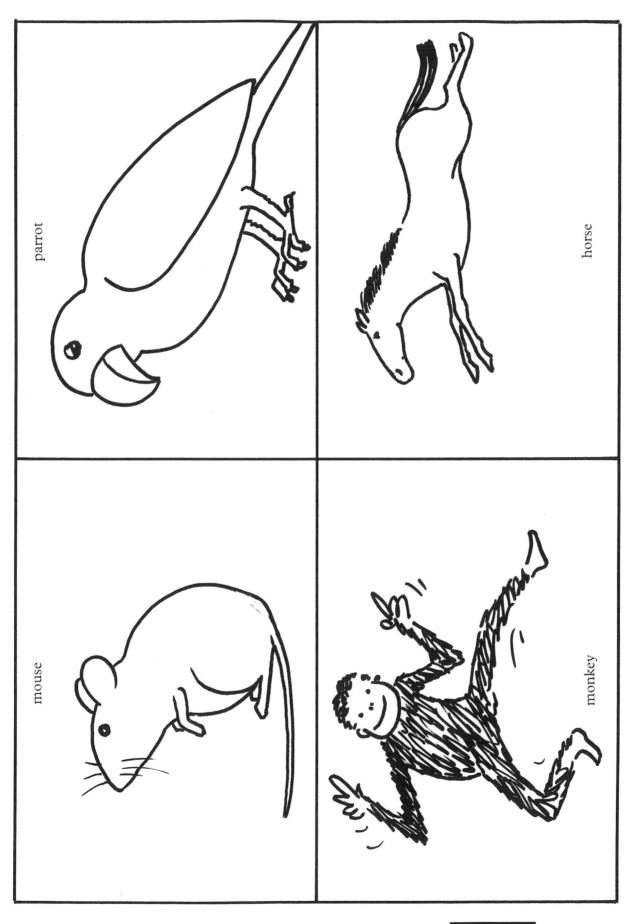

parrot

horse

mouse

monkey

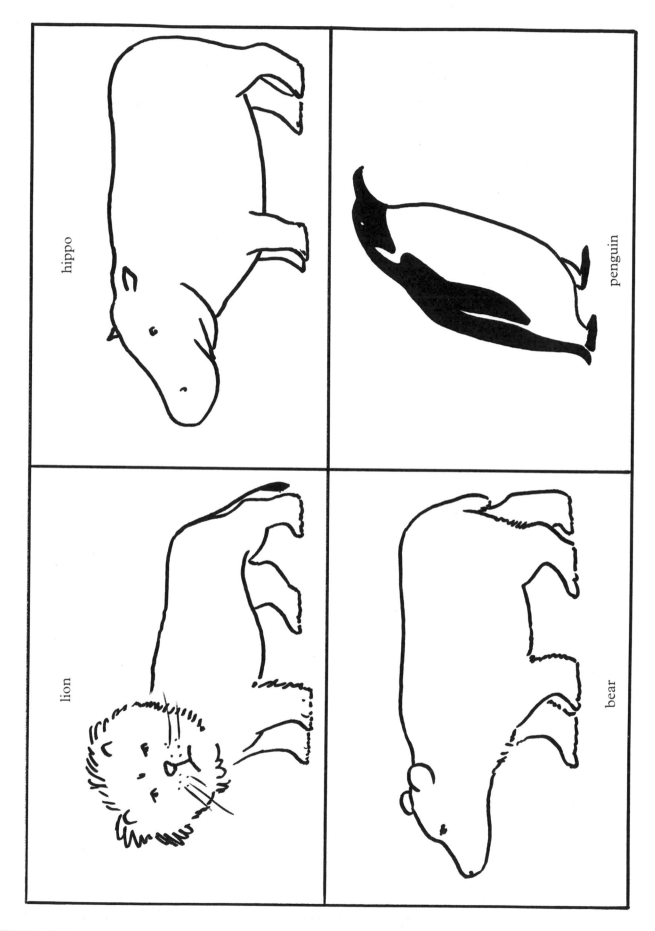

hippo

penguin

lion

bear

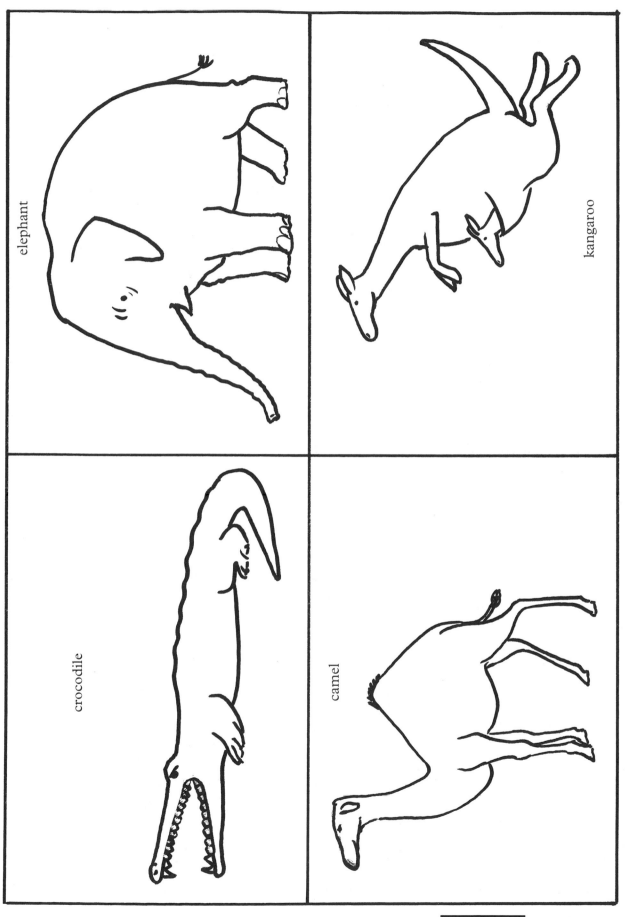

elephant

kangaroo

crocodile

camel

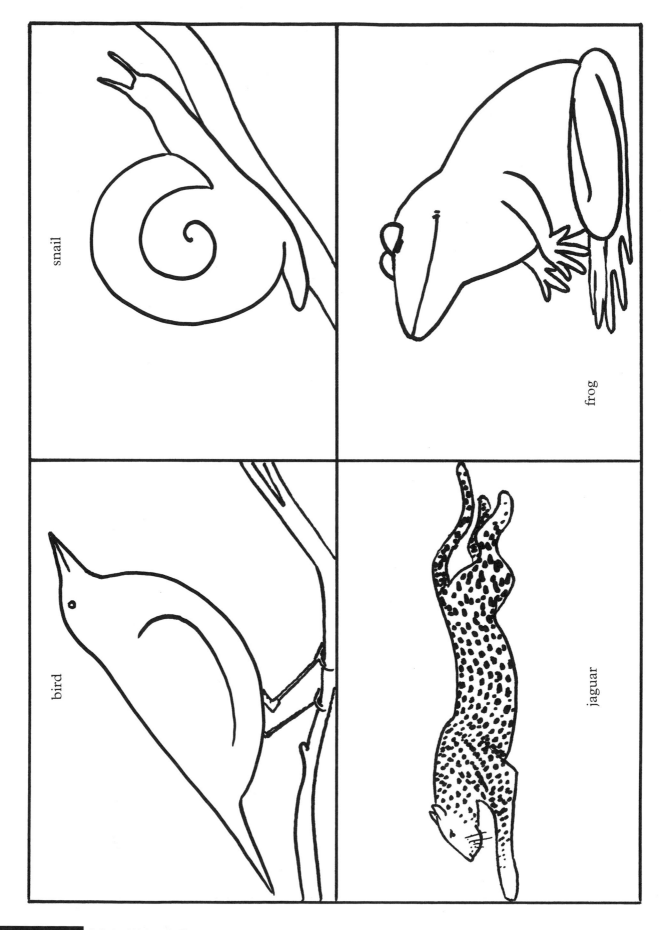

snail

frog

bird

jaguar

shop

street

house

car

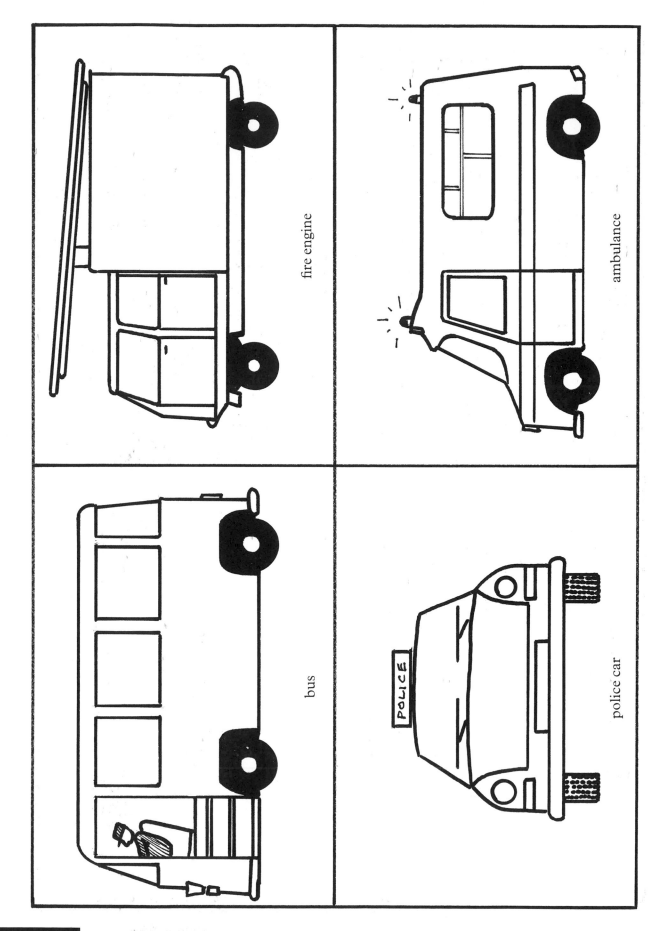

fire engine

ambulance

bus

police car

train

board game

doll

puppet

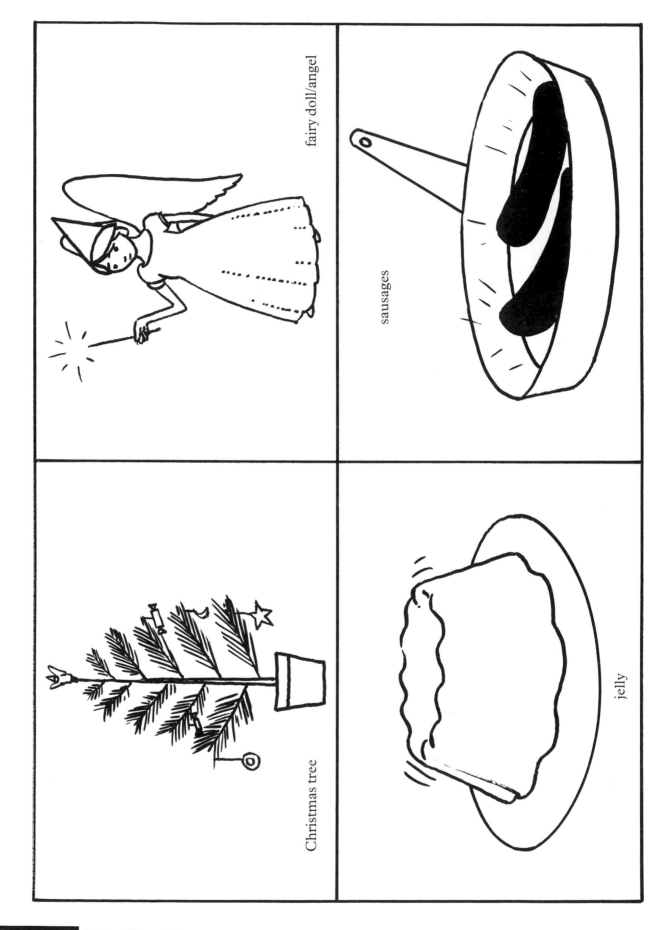

fairy doll/angel

sausages

Christmas tree

jelly

Further reading

Teachers' resources

Language Through Play. 1991. 'Learn Through Play' series. Croydon, U.K.: Pre-school Playgroups Association. ISBN 0 901755 96 6. One of a series of very useful publications for teachers of pre-school children published by the Pre-School Learning Alliance (see below for mail order address).

Bruce, T. 1987. *Early Childhood Education*. London: Hodder and Stoughton. ISBN 0 340 40735 2. A very readable book covering some of the main issues in pre-school teaching.

Hughes, G. S. 1981. *A Handbook of Classroom English*. Oxford: Oxford University Press. ISBN 0 19 431633 5. Useful examples of classroom language with amusing cartoons.

Phillips, S. 1993. *Young Learners*. Oxford: Oxford University Press. ISBN 0 19 437195 6. Resource Books for Teachers series. Advice and activities on teaching English to children aged 6 to 12.

Salaberri, S. 1993. *Classroom English*. Oxford: Heinemann. ISBN 435 282 431. Useful examples of classroom language.

Toth, M. 1995. *Children's Games*. Oxford: Heinemann. ISBN 0435 29466 0. Sixteen games with photocopiable worksheets.

Watts, E. 1995 (new edition). *The Blackboard Book*. London: Sangam Books. ISBN 086311 502 0. Ideas for teachers with few resources, including how to draw on the blackboard.

Wright, A. 1993. (new edition). *1000+ Pictures for Teachers to Copy*. Harlow, Essex, U.K.: Longman. ISBN 017 556878 2. Tips on how to draw quickly and effectively on the board.

Wright, A. 1995. *Storytelling with Children*. Oxford: Oxford University Press. ISBN 0 19 437202 2. Resource Books for Teachers series. Over 30 stories and ideas on exploiting them in class.

Wright, A. 1997. *Creating Stories with Children*. Oxford: Oxford University Press. ISBN 0 19 437204 9. Resource Books for Teachers series. Ideas for helping children tell and write stories in English.

Story-books

These books have been chosen for their appeal to young children, the quality of their pictures, and their clear, simple language, as well as of course a good story.

Ahlberg, J. and **J. Ahlberg.** 1978. *Each Peach Pear Plum*. Harmondsworth, U.K.: Penguin. ISBN 014 050919 4. A rhyming book which encourages observation and includes characters from traditional stories.

Bradman, T. and **M. Chamberlain.** 1989. *Look Out! He's Behind You!* London: Mammoth. ISBN 07497 0024. A lift-the-flap version of the traditional story 'Little Red Riding Hood'.

Campbell, R. 1982. *Dear Zoo.* Harmondsworth, U.K.: Penguin. ISBN 014 050444 6. A lift-the-flap book about a boy trying to choose a suitable pet.

Campbell, R. 1988. *Buster Gets Dressed.* London: Campbell Books/Macmillan. ISBN 0333 65370 X.

Campbell, R. 1988. *My Presents.* London: Campbell Books/Macmillan. ISBN 0 333 59765 6. A lift-the-flap book about a birthday.

Campbell, R. 1994. *Henry's Ball.* London: Campbell Books/Macmillan. ISBN 0 333 61205 1. A 'hide and seek' book.

Carle, E. 1970. *The Very Hungry Caterpillar.* Harmondsworth, U.K.: Penguin. ISBN 014 050087 1. Both entertaining and educational. Available in several languages and in bilingual versions. Also available on video.

Cousins, L. 1990. *Maisy Goes Swimming.* London: Walker Books. ISBN 0 745 0428 7.

Cousins, L. 1992. *Maisy Goes to Playschool.* London: Walker Books. ISBN 0 7445 2506 3.

Cousins, L. 1992. *Maisy Goes to the Playground.* London: Walker Books. ISBN 0 7445 2507 1.

Cousins, L. 1995. *Maisy's House.* London: Walker Books. ISBN 0 7445 4412 2. Simple board books about everyday children's experiences. Excellent teaching aids.

Hill, E. 1983. *Where's Spot?* Harmondsworth, U.K.: Penguin. ISBN 014 050420 6. A well-known lift-the-flap book about a dog hiding. Available in many languages.

Hill, E. 1985. *Spot's Birthday.* Harmondsworth, U.K.: Penguin. ISBN 014 050495 8.

Hindley, L. 1995. *The Big Red Bus.* London: Walker Books. ISBN 07445 4758 X. The big red bus goes over lots of bumps!

Hutchins, P. 1970. *Rosie's Walk.* Harmondsworth, U.K.: Penguin. ISBN 014 050032 4. Rosie the hen goes for a walk but does not know the fox is following her. A very funny book.

Hutchins, P. 1974. *The Wind Blew.* London: Red Fox. ISBN 009 920751 6. A funny story which graphically illustrates the weather.

Jonas, A. 1989. *Colour Dance.* London: Julia McRae. ISBN 086203 452 6. Dancers trail different coloured gauze, mixing colours in fascinating ways.

Lloyd, D. and **L. Voce.** 1989. *Hello, Goodbye.* London: Walker Books. ISBN 07445 1348 0. A simple story about wildlife, greetings, and weather.

Lloyd, E. 1978. *Nini at Carnival.* London: Red Fox. ISBN 009 950181 3. Nini wants to join the parade but has no carnival costume.

Paul, K., V. Thomas, and **J. Cadwallader.** 1995. *Winnie the Witch*. Oxford: Oxford University Press. ISBN 0 19 43904 0. Winnie can't find her black cat in her black house. Specially adapted for children learning English. Teacher's notes, video, CD-ROM, and cassette available.

Rosen, M. and **H. Oxenbury.** 1989. *We're Going On a Bear Hunt*. London: Walker Books. ISBN 07445 2323 0. An illustrated version of a well-known rhyme, which children can act out.

Stickland, P. and **H. Stickland.** 1996. *Dinosaur Roar!* Harmondsworth, U.K.: Penguin. ISBN 014 055702 4. A book of 'opposites'.

Songs and rhymes

Matterson, E. M. (ed.). 1991. *This Little Puffin*. Harmondsworth, U.K.: Penguin. ISBN 0 14 034048 3. Action songs, finger plays, rhymes, etc. with music and illustrations of movements.

Hammond, L. 1990. *Five Furry Teddy Bears*. Harmondsworth, U.K.: Penguin. ISBN 0 14 034151 X. Contemporary action rhymes, finger plays, songs, and games, with music and drawings.

Mother Goose. 1991. London: Walker Books. ISBN 07445 0775 8. A book of traditional nursery rhymes.

Cassettes

Byrne, J. and **A. Waugh.** 1981. *Jingle Bells*. Oxford: Oxford University Press. ISBN 0 19 433345 0 (song book), ISBN 019 433346 9 (cassette). Cassette and book of traditional songs. Contains some of the songs in this book.

Hop, Skip, and Jump. Early Learning Centre. 22 action songs with words and instructions. (For mail order address see below.)

King, K. and **I. Beck.** 1985. *Oranges and Lemons*. Oxford: Oxford University Press. ISBN 019 279985 1 (cassette with song book). Cassette and book of traditional songs for young children, with music and illustrations.

Super Songs. 1997. Oxford: Oxford University Press. ISBN 019 433627 1. Cassette and book of 27 traditional songs. Contains many of the songs in this book. Specially produced for young children learning English.

Tommy Thumb. Early Learning Centre. ISBN. 24 hand action songs including some of those in this book. (See the end of this section for mail order address.)

Williams, S. and **I. Beck.** 1983. *Round and Round the Garden*. Oxford: Oxford University Press. ISBN 0 19 279987 8 (cassette with song book). Cassette and book of finger plays and rhymes for young children, with music and illustrations.

Arts and crafts

The Farm, The Sea, The Street Where I Live, The Zoo. 'Creative Sticker Fun' series. Bridlington, U.K.: Peter Haddock Ltd. ISBN 0 7105 0668 6. A delightful set of books with reusable stickers which enable children to create their own pictures. They are very useful for learning vocabulary and for creating stories.

Bartlett, N. L. 1986. *Children's Art and Crafts*. Sydney: Australian Women's Weekly Home Library. ISBN 0 949128 42 2. A marvellous, comprehensive collection of art and craft activities for children aged 2 to 8: pictures, puppets, cookery, sculpture, festival crafts, etc. With colour photos.

Gee, R. 1986. *Entertaining and Educating Young Children*. London: Usborne. ISBN 0 86020 943 1.

Gee, R. 1986. *Entertaining and Educating Your Preschool Child*. London: Usborne. ISBN 0 7460 0133 9.

Moxley, J. 1993. *'She' 150 Things to Make and Do With Your Children*. London: Vermilion. ISBN 009 177760 7.

Smith, J. 1993. *Good Housekeeping Kids' Cook Book*. London: Ebury Press. ISBN 009 178072 1. A first step-by-step guide for young cooks. Fun recipes, both savoury and sweet. Clear instructions and photos.

Posters

Brockhampton Press:

My First Nursery Rhymes ISBN 1 86019 260 2.

Transport 1 86019 226 2.

Walker Books:

Posters from book illustrations; for mail order address see below.

McDonnell, F. *I Love Animals*

Foreman, M. *Nursery Rhymes*

Lacome, J. *Humpty Dumpty and Other Rhymes*

Burningham, J. *Colours*

Early Childhood Publications Pte Ltd.: Singapore, Fax (+65) 274 6789:

In the Park ISBN 981 209 378 8.

Wild Animals ISBN 981 209 599 3.

Transport ISBN 981 209 325 7.

Videos

Children's TV Favourites Volume 1 and 2. Abbey Home Entertainment. NSPCC 90472. A collection of popular children's programmes, sold in aid of a children's charity. Includes Postman Pat, Spot the Dog, and other well-known characters.

Favourite Fairy Tales Video Series. Harlow, Essex, U.K.: Longman. A collection of Hans Christian Andersen stories. There is an accompanying collection of illustrated books.

The Greatest BBC Children's Video Ever. BBCV 5653. Another collection of popular pre-school children's programmes.

Muzzy in Gondoland. BBC. Produced specially for children learning English.

Pingu's Big Video. Tempo Pre-school. BBCV 5460. Fifteen short stories about the little penguin.

Spot and Friends. King Rollo Films Ltd., London.

Wizadora. Oxford: Oxford University Press. A young wizard makes lots of mistakes. Made for children learning English. Teacher's guide and audio cassette available.

Mail order addresses

Early Learning Centre, Mail Order Dept., South Marston Park, Swindon SN3 4TJ, U.K. Tel. (+44) (0)1793 444844. Educational books, videos, cassettes, puppets, games, puzzles, etc. for the pre-school child. Can deliver most products anywhere in the world.

Pre-School Learning Alliance M. H., 45–49 Union Road, Croydon, Surrey CRO 2XL, U.K. Tel. 0181 684 9542. Will send items by mail order to any country.

Walker Books Ltd., BBCS, PO Box 941, Hull, North Humberside, HU1 3YQ, UK. Will send books to other countries. 24 hour credit card tel.: (+44) (0)1482 224626.

Other titles in the Resource Books for Teachers series

Beginners, by Peter Grundy—communicative activities for both absolute and 'false' beginners, including those who do not know the Roman alphabet. All ages. (ISBN 0 19 437200 6)

Class Readers, by Jean Greenwood—activities to develop extensive and intensive reading skills, plus listening and speaking tasks. All ages. (ISBN 0 19 437103 4)

Classroom Dynamics, by Jill Hadfield—helps teachers maintain a good working relationship with their classes and so promote effective learning. Teenagers and adults. (ISBN 0 19 437147 6)

Conversation, by Rob Nolasco and Lois Arthur—over 80 activities to develop students' ability to speak confidently and fluently. Teenagers and adults. (ISBN 0 19 437096 8)

Creating Stories with Children, by Andrew Wright—encourages creativity, confidence, and fluency and accuracy in spoken and written English. Age 7–14. (ISBN 0 19 437204 9)

Cultural Awareness, by Barry Tomalin and Susan Stempleski—challenges stereotypes, using cultural issues as a rich resource for language practice. Teenagers and adults. (ISBN 0 19 437194 8)

Dictionaries, by Jonathan Wright—ideas for making more effective use of dictionaries in class. Teenagers and adults. (ISBN 019 437219 7)

Drama, by Charlyn Wessels—creative and enjoyable activities using drama to teach spoken communication skills and literature. Teenagers and adults. (ISBN 0 19 437097 6)

Drama with Children, by Sarah Phillips—practical ideas to develop speaking skills, self-confidence, imagination, and creativity. Age 6–12. (ISBN 0 19 437220 0)

Exam Classes, by Peter May—preparation for a wide variety of public examinations, including most of the main American and British exams. Teenagers and adults. (ISBN 0 19 437208 1)

Games for Children, by Gordon Lewis with Günther Bedson—an exciting collection of games for children aged 4–12. (ISBN 0 19 437224 3)

Grammar Dictation, by Ruth Wajnryb—the 'dictogloss' technique—improves understanding and use of grammar by reconstructing texts. Teenagers and adults. (ISBN 0 19 437004 6)

The Internet, by David Eastment, David Hardisty, and Scott Windeatt—motivates learners and brings a wealth of material into the classroom. For all levels of expertise. Teenagers and adults. (ISBN 0 19 437223 5)

Learner-based Teaching, by Colin Campbell and Hanna Kryszewska—unlocks the wealth of knowledge that learners bring to the classroom. All ages. (ISBN 0 19 437163 8)

Letters, by Nicky Burbidge, Peta Gray, Sheila Levy, and Mario Rinvolucri—using letters and e-mail for language and cultural study. Teenagers and adults. (ISBN 0 19 442149 X)

Listening, by Goodith White—advice and ideas for encouraging learners to become 'active listeners'. Teenagers and adults. (ISBN 0 19 437216 2)

Literature, by Alan Maley and Alan Duff—an innovatory book on using literature for language practice. Teenagers and adults. (ISBN 0 19 437094 1)

Music and Song, by Tim Murphey—'tuning in' to students' musical tastes can increase motivation and tap a rich vein of resources. All ages. (ISBN 0 19 437055 0)

Newspapers, by Peter Grundy—original ideas for making effective use of newspapers in lessons. Teenagers and adults. (ISBN 0 19 437192 6)

Projects with Young Learners, by Diane Phillips, Sarah Burwood, and Helen Dunford—encourages learner independence by producing a real sense of achievement. Age 5 to 13 (ISBN 0 19 437221 9)

Project Work, by Diana L. Fried-Booth—bridges the gap between the classroom and the outside world. Teenagers and adults. (ISBN 0 19 437092 5)

Pronunciation, by Clement Laroy—imaginative activities to build confidence and improve all aspects of pronunciation. All ages. (ISBN 0 19 437087 9)

Role Play, by Gillian Porter Ladousse—controlled conversations to improvised drama, simple dialogues to complex scenarios. Teenagers and adults. (ISBN 0 19 437095 X)

Self-Access, by Susan Sheerin—advice on setting up and managing self-access study facilities, plus materials. Teenagers and adults. (ISBN 0 19 437099 2)

Storytelling with Children, by Andrew Wright—hundreds of exciting ideas for using any story to teach English to children aged 7 to 14. (ISBN 0 19 437202 2)

Translation, by Alan Duff—a wide variety of translation activities from many different subject areas. Teenagers and adults. (ISBN 0 19 437104 2)

Video, by Richard Cooper, Mike Lavery, and Mario Rinvolucri—original ideas for watching and making videos. All ages. (ISBN 0 19 437102 6)

Vocabulary, by John Morgan and Mario Rinvolucri—a wide variety of communicative activities for teaching new words. Teenagers and adults. (ISBN 437091 7)

Writing, by Tricia Hedge—a wide range of writing tasks, as well as guidance on student difficulties with writing. Teenagers and adults. (ISBN 0 19 437098 4)

Young Learners, by Sarah Phillips—advice and ideas for teaching English to children aged 6–12, including arts and crafts, games, stories, poems, and songs. (ISBN 0 19 437195 6)

Index

Topics

animals 3.11, 3.21, 3.22, 5.5, 5.7, 5.10, 5.15, 5.16, 5.19, 5.20, 6.14, 6.15
birthdays 3.3, 3.21, 3.22
body 2.6, 2.7, 3.4, 3.10, 3.12, 3.19, 3.23, 3.24, 3.27, 3.28
Carnival 6.11
Christmas 6.1, 6.2, 6.3, 6.4, 6.5, 6.7, 6.8, 6.9, 6.10
clothes 5.14
colours 1.4, 3.17, 3.23, 4.5, 4.6, 4.7, 4.9. 4.13, 4.14. 4.15, 5.2, 5.12, 6.6, 6.7, 6.15, 6.18
Easter 6.13, 6.16
emergency services 5.3, 5.13
fairy tales 1.3
family 3.9, 3.16, 3.25, 3.26
feelings 3.5
food 3.8, 3.13, 3.24, 6.13
health 5.9, 5.11
introductions 3.2
likes and dislikes 3.8, 3.11, 3.13, 3.15, 3.17
monsters 1.5
pirates 6.12
road safety 5.2
robots 3.7, 3.18, 3.27
shapes 2.10, 4.9, 4.16, 6.6
time 4.10
towns 5.1, 5.6
toys 3.1, 3.2, 3.6, 3.15, 6.3
traffic 5.12
transport 3.9, 3.26
video 1.2, 3.22
weather 4.6, 5.4, 5.7, 5.8, 5.14, 5.17, 6.2

Cross-curricular themes

art and craft 3.23, 3.24, 3.25, 3.26, 3.27, 3.28, 3.29, 4.12, 4.13, 4.14, 4.15, 4.16, 5.7, 5.17, 5.18, 5.19, 5.20, 6.7, 6.8, 6.10, 6.12, 6.15, 6.18
balls 2.1, 2.2
calming activities 2.8, 2.9, 2.10, 2.11
classifying 2.8, 4.14
co-operation 1.3, 1.4
co-ordination 1.4, 2.1, 2.2, 3.4, 3.14, 3.15, 3.19, 3.20, 3.23, 3.26, 3.27, 3.28, 3.29, 4.8, 4.12, 4.13, 4.16, 5.17, 5.18, 5.19, 5.20, 6.7, 6.8, 6.10, 6.12, 6.15, 6.17, 6.18
cognitive development 2.8, 2.10, 2.11
confidence-building 3.1, 6.9
cookery 3.28
drama and role-play 1.3, 3.21, 3.22, 5.11, 6.9
drawing 1.5, 2.6, 3.11, 3.15, 3.25
games 2.7, 3.18, 3.19, 4.7, 4.8, 4.9, 4.10, 5.11, 5.12, 5.13, 5.14, 6.6, 6.17
motor skills 2.1
movement and mime 2.2, 3.4, 3.5, 3.7, 3.8, 3.9, 3.11, 3.12, 3.13, 3.21, 4.2, 4.3, 4.4, 5.1, 5.2, 5.4, 5.5, 5.6, 5.7, 5.8, 6.1, 6.2, 6.4, 6.11, 6.15
pencil control 1.6
photographs 1.6
puppets 3.1, 3.2, 3.29
rhymes 3.12, 3.13, 3.14, 5.6, 5.7, 5.8, 5.9, 5.10, 6.4, 6.5
songs 3.1, 3.2, 3.3, 3.4, 3.5, 3.6, 3.7, 3.8, 3.9, 3.10, 3.11, 4.1, 4.2, 4.3, 4.4, 4.5, 4.6, 5.1, 5.2, 5.3, 5.4, 5.5, 6.1, 6.2, 6.3, 6.11, 6.13
stories 1.2, 3.20, 3.21, 4.11, 5.1, 5.16, 6.14
storybooks 1.1
Total Physical Response 3.2, 3.4, 3.5, 3.7, 3.8, 3.9, 3.10, 3.11, 3.12, 3.13, 3.18, 3.20, 4.2, 4.4, 5.1, 5.2, 5.3, 5.4, 5.5, 5.6, 5.7, 5.8, 5.9, 5.12, 5.13, 5.14, 5.15
visual recognition 2.8, 2.9, 2.10, 2.11

Language

action verbs 3.7, 3.18, 3.20, 3.29, 5.1, 5.5, 5.15, 6.17

adjectives 5.5

be 2.1, 2.6, 2.8, 2.10, 2.11, 3.1, 3.2, 3.3, 3.4, 3.5, 3.7, 3.21, 3.23, 3.25, 4.13, 4.14, 4.15, 4.16, 5.5, 5.8. 5.13, 5.14, 6.3, 6.4, 6.6, 6.14, 6.15, 6.16, 6.18

can (**ability**) 3.7

can (**permission**) 4.7

comparatives 5.16

could you ...? 2.4

going to 4.11, 6.11

have got 3.11, 3.16, 3.17, 4.8

how old are you? 3.3

imperatives 2.2, 2.3, 2.5, 2.6, 2.7, 2.9, 4.4

instructions 1.4, 2.2, 2.3, 2.4, 2.5, 2.6, 2.7, 2.8, 2.9, 2.10, 2.11, 3.10, 3.16, 3.17, 3.18, 3.23, 3.24, 3.26, 3.27, 3.28, 3.29, 4.4, 4.12, 4.13, 4.14, 4.16, 5.12, 5.14, 5.15, 5.17, 5.18, 5.19, 5.20, 6.8, 6.9, 6.10, 6.12, 6.13, 6.17, 6.18

left/right 3.10

love ... 3.6

names 1.4, 1.6, 2.2, 3.1

numbers 3.3, 3.8, 3.19, 3.21, 3.22, 4.1, 4.2, 4.3, 4.4, 4.10

past simple 4.2, 4.11, 5.7, 5.9

prepositions 5.1, 5.6, 5.7, 6.16

present continuous 4.4

pronunciation 3.14, 5.6, 5.10

question and answer 2.1

stress/rhythm 3.13, 3.14, 3.15, 5.1, 6.5, 6.11

what is it? 6.6

where is/are ...? 1.4, 3.2, 3.21, 3.22, 6.16

who's ...? 3.22

will/won't 4.11

OXFORD
UNIVERSITY PRESS

Dear Teacher

We would like your views on how best to develop the *Resource Books for Teachers* series. We would be very grateful if you could fill in this questionnaire and return it to the address at the bottom. We are offering a free OUP wallchart to everyone who returns this form, and a free Resource Book each for the ten most informative replies received every month.

About yourself

Your name ————————————————————————

Address ————————————————————————

————————————————————————

————————————————————————

Are you: ☐ A teacher?   ☐ A teacher trainer?   ☐ A trainee teacher?

Other? (Please specify) ————————————————————

What type of establishment do you work in? ————————————

What age are your students?   ☐ 3–6   ☐ 6–12   ☐ 12–17   ☐ 18+

How many students per class?   ☐ under 15   ☐ 15–30   ☐ over 30

Which teachers' resource book(s) do you use most (from any publisher)?

————————————————————————

Which topic(s) would you most like to have covered in a Resource Book for Teachers?

————————————————————————

————————————————————————

About *Very Young Learners*

Do you read the Introduction? Yes/No

Do you find it useful? Why? ————————————————

————————————————————————

Which activities do you find most useful? Why?

————————————————————————

————————————————————————

Is there anything you **don't** like about the book? ————————

————————————————————————

We have changed the size of this book and hope you like it and the new cover design.

Which size do you prefer?   ☐ This size   ☐ Don't mind

☐ Other? (Please specify) ————————————————

Do you photocopy the worksheets?   Yes/No

Any other comments? (*You can continue your comments on a separate sheet if you wish.*)

————————————————————————

————————————————————————

————————————————————————

————————————————————————

Please send your reply to:
Julia Sallabank
Senior Editor, ELT
Oxford University Press
Great Clarendon Street
Oxford
OX2 6DP
UK

Thank you very much for taking the time to answer this questionnaire.

Which wallchart would you prefer?

☐ Map of the UK and world   ☐ The zany zoo (primary)

☐ Map of the USA   ☐ Town scene with worksheets (primary)

☐ English sounds (IPA symbols)

Which Resource Book for Teachers would you prefer? (See the list on pages 191–3.)